Brooches
and
Badges

ACCESSORIES

Brooches and Badges

Rachel Church

Thames & Hudson | V&A

Contents

Introduction

The history of the brooch, and its design, are inseparable from the history and design of dress. Brooches began their life as practical garment fasteners (see pp. 6–7), and their use has risen and fallen as changes in fashion have made them more or less wearable. From the earliest years, jewellers and goldsmiths took this necessary dress fastener and turned it into a work of art, whether the stamped gold of the Etruscan fibula (**1**) or the garnet mosaic of the Anglo-Saxon circular brooch (**2**). Unlike other types of jewellery, such as rings or earrings, brooches are essentially mobile. They can be pinned to clothing on the breast, shoulder, back or waist; sometimes their owners also fixed them to hats, bags and shoes.

Jewellers have taken this basic function and used it to create jewels of endless variety, in materials ranging from the most prized to the most mundane. But jewellery has always been far more than decoration. As the *Goldsmiths' Journal* explained in 1926: 'Jewellery is worn because of its use as a historic and social convention (witness the engagement ring and wedding ring). It is worn for joy and it is worn for vanity. It is bought as a sacred rite, it is bought as a social and domestic duty, it is bought under compulsion, it is bought as a bribe and it is bought in a delirium…'.[1]

Beyond both their utilitarian and decorative purposes, brooches, badges, clips and pins served to create and communicate an identity. Whether the medieval pilgrim badge, the Victorian cameo brooch, the twentieth-century political pin or the avant-garde works of modern craft jewellers, these objects speak to us down the years. Although the roles of the brooch as a dress fastener and an often gorgeous form of adornment are key, perhaps more than any other form of jewellery the pin is an expression of belonging, official or not. Wearing a brooch or badge can be a way of asking and sometimes answering those vital questions: Who am I? What do I represent?

The selection of brooches found in this book, based on the collections of the Victoria and Albert Museum, will allow us to begin to address such questions, giving us a way into these fascinating jewels without pretending to offer definitive answers, in what is a sumptuous, complex and richly rewarding field.

1 Stamped gold. Tuscany (Etruria), 550–500 BC.
8841-1863

2 Garnet, gold and shell. Kent, England, AD 600–700.
M.109-1939

CHAPTER ONE

'Send...letters, tokens, brooches, and rynges'
1000–1500

Brooches in the medieval period had several overlapping functions. They served to secure dress, to signal the wearer's identity and political loyalties, and to be given as symbols of love and friendship. As with all jewels, they were also beautiful, decorative objects that completed a well-dressed, appropriate appearance.

However, the primary function of a medieval brooch was as a dress fastener. Until the development of buttons, which were not widely used until the 14th century, brooches were used to hold layers of fabric together on long and loosely fitted garments. Brooches served to fasten the neck opening of tunics and to clasp cloaks, and they were often arranged decoratively down the bodice. A limestone statue of a king, from the High Cross formerly situated in Bristol marketplace, shows two very large star-shaped brooches pinned to the front of his chest (**4**). Brooches could also be used to attach small personal items such as rosary beads, purses and aprons to clothing, or to close the flap of a cloth bag.[1]

'I have brooches of gilt brass and of silvered latten, and so fond are folk of latten that often it is valued as silver', proclaims the Mercier, or travelling mercer-peddler, in the short poem 'Le Dit du Mercier'.[2] In an illustration from the Codex Manesse (**3**), the poet Dietmar von Aist takes the guise of a peddler to offer a ring brooch to his lover. A selection of his other goods, including girdles and bags, hangs behind him.

As the 13th-century Mercier's song suggests, the most common materials used in medieval brooches were metals. Gold, silver and silver-gilt were favoured for the most expensive jewels. Gold was by far the most valuable, costing ten times as much as silver. For this reason, many of the largest brooches were melted down for the value of the metal or later remade into a more fashionable jewel. Cheaper versions were made in bronze, pewter and latten, copying the designs of gold and silver brooches. Colour was sometimes added through bright enamelling, traces of which survive on some jewels. Pearls provided brightness and light, while some brooches were set with hardstone cameos. The most valuable brooches were set with polished gemstones (see **7** and **8**) or reused classical intaglios and cameos. Brooches could also be set with enamelled images, showing religious scenes or images from Greek or Roman mythology. Gold and gem-set brooches were made for individual customers, but the Mercier's lay makes it clear that cheaper jewels could be bought ready-made from travelling salesmen. Casting brooches in reusable stone moulds made a degree of mass production possible.

The ring brooch is by far the most common type of medieval brooch in the V&A collection: a simple, usually circular jewel with a pin across the centre which was passed through fabric so that the pull of the cloth against the pin held the brooch in place. These were widely worn from the late 12th to the 15th century. From around 1300, ring brooches could be made in

3 Dietmar von Aist offers a brooch to his lover.
Miniature from the Codex Manesse, Zurich, c.1300–40.

heart, flower, rectangular and lozenge shapes (**5** and **10**). Although most were clearly functional, some brooches are so small that they must have been purely decorative. A tiny, double-ended gem-set brooch (**6**) can only have held the lightest of fabrics, perhaps closing the collar of an open-necked gown. The gold is finely cast with decorative animal heads and rosettes, and set with small imitation emeralds and a fine sapphire, suggesting that it was owned by a person of high social standing. The sapphire was not only a valuable, princely stone; for the original owner it would also have held the power to cure ulcers, protect the eyes, promote devotion and, according to the poem *Piers Plowman*, destroy 'envenymes [venoms]'.[3]

The basic outline of the brooch was often embellished by engraving or added decoration. The stone collets on one brooch (**7**) are circled with naturalistic grape vines and leaves in the Gothic style, while another brooch (**8**) is set with tiny golden flowers. Cabochon gemstones were often set in gold collars, and mottoes or phrases in engraved scrolls combined meaning with ornament.

Many ring brooches were engraved with romantic inscriptions, often in French, the language of courtly love, such as *sans departir* ('without parting') and *vous et nul autre* ('you and no other'). The peddler in John Heywood's 1544 play holds items vital for those who 'love would win', including 'brooches, rings, and all manner [of] beads'.[4] Indeed, if you would serve your lady, you must 'send [her] letters, tokens, brooches, and rynges' advised Geoffrey Chaucer's narrator in 1385.[5] Jewellery, especially rings and ring brooches, was a common gift between lovers and friends, and courtship at all levels of society involved the exchange of gifts of both great and small value. Brooches also formed part of elaborate gift exchanges at New Year celebrations.

4 Figure of a king, limestone. England, c.1400.
LOAN: National Trust.5

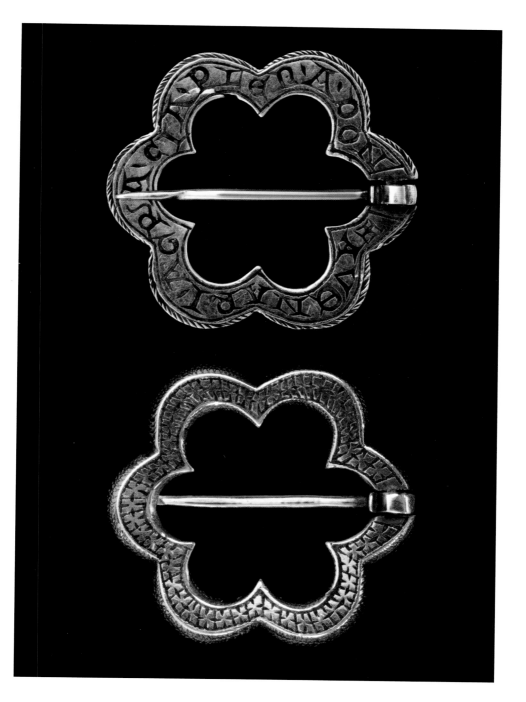

5 Gold and enamel, engraved *Ave Maria Gracia Plena Don*.
Possibly England or France, 1250–1350.
M.245-1923

6 Gold, sapphire and green pastes. England, 1200–1300.
M.26-1993. Purchased with Art Fund support and assistance from the Murray Bequest

7 Gold, garnets, sapphires and niello. France, 1225–75.
547-1897

8 Gold, garnets and sapphires. France or England, 1250–1300.
M.530-1910. Salting Bequest

Marriage was vitally important in ensuring the safe transfer of property to legitimate heirs. As a valid marriage could be formed at this time simply by two lovers exchanging vows, without the involvement of church or state, rituals such as the exchange of gifts became especially important. Offering or accepting a token such as a ring or ring brooch and wearing it openly could form a public acknowledgment of a legally binding contract. In a miniature illustrating Gratian's law text (**9**), the woman in the couple on the left-hand side of the image has accepted the large ring brooch that is being proffered and is openly affectionate. On the right-hand side, the gift appears to have been declined or returned and the man is turning away in disappointment.

The message of love is reinforced on two heart-shaped brooches, which would originally have been coloured with enamel. Engraved with a pattern of feathers around the front, one bears the inscription *Nostre et tout ditz a vostre desier* ('Ourselves and all things as you desire') on the reverse, signifying the gift of not only the brooch, but also the loyalty and love of the donor (**10**). The other, still retaining traces of white enamel (**11**), and a circular brooch (**12**), are both inscribed with a version of *sans departir*, possibly an abbreviated version of the motto on another heart-shaped brooch, found as part of the 15th-century Fishpool hoard (now at the British Museum), which is inscribed *Je suy vostre sans de partier* ('I am yours without parting').

9 Ring brooches being exchanged between lovers. Miniature illustration from *Decretum Gratiani*, c.1300–1400. Photo: Bibliothèque nationale de France, MS. Lat. 3898, folio 361r

10 Gold, engraved *Nostre et tout ditz a vostre desier*.
Possibly France or England, c.1400.
86-1899

11 Gold, engraved *Sans departier*.
Possibly England or France, c.1400–25.
M.40-1975. Given by Dame Joan Evans

12 Gold, engraved 'canc d/epaer/tir', a version of *sans departir*.
England or France, c.1400.
M.44-1975. Given by Dame Joan Evans

13 Gold, engraved *Non detur petenti*. England or France, 1200–1300.
M.43-1975. Given by Dame Joan Evans

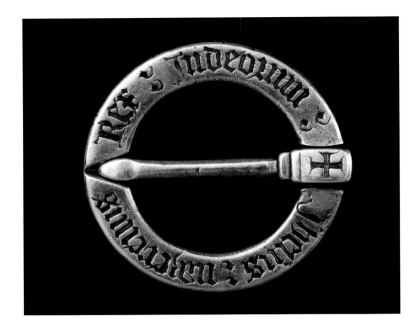

Chaucer's tragic romance *Troilus and Criseyde* uses the exchange and transfer of brooches to show how the heroine's affections change throughout the story. At the beginning of the romance, Criseyde gifts a 'brooch, gold and azure', in which a ruby 'like a heart' was set, which she pins to Troilus's shirt. On leaving Troy, he reciprocates with a brooch to remember him by, which she promises to keep always. However, the faithless Criseyde does not fulfil this promise and the brooch is later seen fixed to her new lover's armour, to Troilus's dismay. Chaucer's audience would clearly have understood both the role of the brooch as a love gift and the way its transfer formed a visual indication of changed affections and allegiance.[6] This interchange of brooches also demonstrates the way in which the brooch was worn by both sexes and could be given as a love gift by either.

While the brooch had a practical use as a dress fastener, its placement at the neckline also served symbolically to protect the virtue of the wearer. This implied message is made explicit on a gold circular brooch with the motto *Non detur petenti* ('Let it not be given up to him that requests it') – a plea for the gift to be preserved, as Criseyde so signally failed to do, as well as for the wearer's modesty to be protected (**13**). The meaning is more explicit in a brooch found at Writtle, Essex, and now in the British Museum, on which is inscribed, in French, 'I am a brooch to guard the breast / that no rascal may put his hand thereon'.[7] The poet Johannes de Hauville put it even more plainly in his 1184 poem *Archithrenius*:

My bride shall wear a brooch – a witness to her modesty and a proof that hers will be a chaste bed. It will shut up her breast and thrust back any intruder, preventing its closed approach from gaping open and the entrance to her bosom from being cheapened by becoming a beaten path for any traveller and an adulterous eye from tasting what delights the honourable caresses of a husband.[8]

14 Silver-gilt, engraved in Latin *Jhesus Nazarenus, Rex Iudeorum* and in English 'John Lamb'. England, 1400–50.
M.12-1969

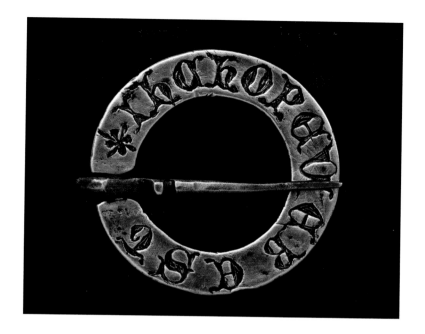

The English author of the 1410 poem *Dives and Pauper* confirmed this view when he described a brooch on the breast as one of the three ornaments of a wife and a token of 'cleanness in heart and chastity'.[9] The heroine of the 13th-century *Romance of the Rose* makes good use of the ambiguous nature of the ring brooch by placing her gold brooch rather low, 'so that an opening, one finger wide, gave a glimpse of her breasts, white as snow on the branches'.[10]

Men also wore brooches to fasten cloaks or the necks of their garments. In Chaucer's 'Monk's Tale', the monk is described as wearing a 'ful curious pyn' in the form of a gold love-knot to fasten his hood[11] – a surprising choice for a monk.

Europe in the Middle Ages was a predominantly Christian society: jewellery engraved with religious mottoes or the figures of saints was worn to show the wearer's Christian identity and to provide protection against physical and spiritual ailments. Ring brooches were engraved

with the salutation of the Angel Gabriel to the Virgin Mary, *Ave Maria gracia plena* ('Hail Mary, full of grace'), or with the name of Jesus, *Jhesus Nazarenus, Rex Iudeorum* ('Jesus of Nazareth, King of the Jews', the phrase or *titulus* that was placed on the upper part of the Crucifix, often abbreviated as INRI) (**14**). These inscriptions would not only prompt the wearer to prayer: such powerful words were moreover believed to form real and effective protection against danger and to ward off illness; they served as a 'divine remedy to protect the faithful in their daily struggle against the Devil'.[12] In particular, the INRI inscription, combined with the names of the Three Kings, was said to cure epileptic fits, while invoking the name of Christ was a protection against sudden death. A silver brooch engraved 'IHC Hope ye best' makes this function clear: the letters IHC, which are an abbreviation of the name of Christ, were combined with a motto encouraging hope and trust (**15**). Another small gold brooch is set with a pair of projecting hands, possibly representing

15 Silver, engraved 'IHC Hope ye best'.
England, 1300–50.
M.47-1975. Given by Dame Joan Evans

prayer (**16**). St George and St Christopher were two of the most popular saints in medieval Europe: George was the patron saint of England, while Christopher protected travellers. A gold brooch engraved with these figures (**17**) may indicate a personal devotion to those saints and a desire to call upon their protective powers, or it could simply refer to the wearer's name. The silver brooch inscribed with the name of Christ (see **14**) also bears the name of its first owner, John Lamb.

Every pilgrimage site had vendors selling pewter, latten or more expensive badges in the form of the pilgrimage site itself, the image of the saint or the saint's emblem. These badges were a public sign that the wearer had completed the pilgrimage and served as protection on the dangerous return journey. In one 15th-century illustration (**18**), a seven-year-old blind boy and his guide wear badges pinned to their hats, indicating that they had carried out several prior pilgrimages before receiving a miraculous

cure at the tomb of St Louis at Saint-Denis in France.

A gold badge in the form of a shield (**19**) is inscribed in French with 'abcd is my lesson', suggesting that it may have been worn by a child. The inscription demonstrates both the use of French as an elite and courtly language in medieval Europe, and the gradual increase in lay literacy: brooches shaped like individual letters and items of dress decorated with letters became commonly worn items. A belt set with the letters of the alphabet, for example, was kept as a relic in Chartres Cathedral and is believed to have been given to St Lubin as a boy to help him learn his letters.[13] There are few surviving shield-shaped brooches, although evidence for their use can be found in funerary monuments. Some circular German ring brooches held an engraved or enamel shield fixed onto the pin, suggesting that the shield brooch from the V&A collection could originally have been part of a similar brooch.[14]

16 Gold. England, or possibly France, 1300–1400.
M.48-1975. Given by Dame Joan Evans

17 Gold, engraved with figures of St George and St Christopher. England, 1350–1400.
2280-1855

18 Miniature on vellum, showing blind pilgrim boy,
from *Le Livre des faiz monseigneur saint Loys*, France, 1401–1500.
Photo: Bibliothèque nationale de France, MS. Français 2829, fol. 102r

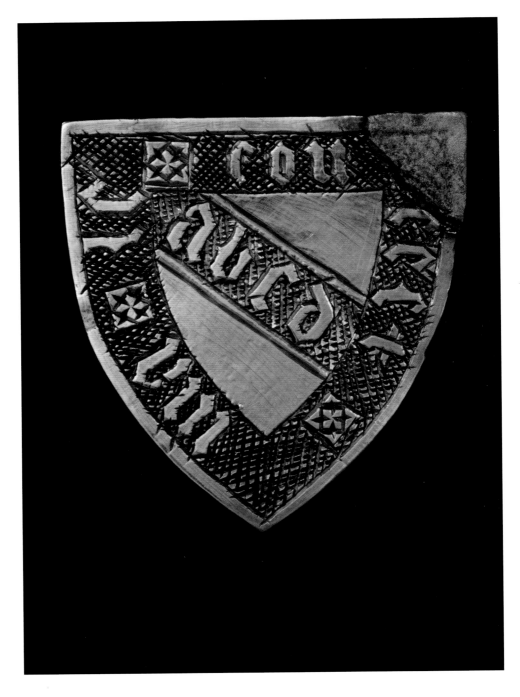

19 Gold, engraved *abcd cest ma lecon*.
Possibly England or France, c.1400.
M.37-1975. Given by Dame Joan Evans

The badge was also an important way to signal allegiance in an age when personal relationships were paramount. From the mid-12th century, the knightly class became a defined and important part of society, and medieval brooches were sometimes decorated with a heraldic badge or device particular to a knightly family.

During the English wars of the 14th century, lords gave badges and clothing decorated with their personal devices to be worn by their retainers and supporters, and even to be attached to their horse harnesses. A copper alloy shield enamelled in the blue and gilt checkerboard pattern of the Warenne family is the kind of badge that may have been fixed to a retainer's horse tack, clothing or belt (**20**). A pewter badge shaped like a curled feather passing through a crown is also thought to be a retainer's badge, possibly associated with the Lancastrian faction in the War of the Roses (**21**). In fact, the practice of giving badges became so associated with political and social instability that parliamentary efforts were made to suppress it.[15]

20 (left) Copper alloy and enamel, with the arms of the Warenne family.
England, 1300–50.
M.13-1989

21 (right) Pewter. England, 1400–1500.
M.64-1980

CHAPTER TWO
'Rich Apparell, precious Jewells'
1500–1800

The development of the button made brooches less important as dress fasteners, although small brooches were still used to pin shirt collars and to fasten slits in the fashionably slashed clothing of the 16th century and the sleeve seams of 17th-century dresses. Instead, jewelled and enamelled hat badges, bows and breast ornaments were stitched or pinned to male and female clothing. This custom – characterized as 'Rich Apparell, precious Jewells'[1] – was part of an overall magnificence of costume, using jewels attached to expensive silks and velvets or fabrics embroidered and enriched with gold and silver lace. To William Harrison, writing about the Tudor court of the 1570s, walking through the crowds was likened 'to the show of a peacock's tail in full beauty, or of some meadow garnished with infinite kind of pleasant flowers'.[2] A system of symbols based on a shared visual language, codified in printed books of emblems such as Cesare Ripa's *Iconologia* of 1593 or Geffrey Witney's 1586 *A Choice of Emblems*, informed designs for jewels, dress and portraiture, and was incorporated into poetry and plays.

Hat badges were a particular, mostly male, form of jewellery. The fashion originated at the French court at the end of the 15th century. One circular gold jewel originally had small loops on the rim so the badge could be stitched to fabric (**23**). This jewel is set with the enamelled, severed head of St John the Baptist, who was beheaded at the request of Salome. A relic of St John's skull was brought back to France by the Crusaders in 1204, and pilgrimages to Amiens in Normandy enabled believers to pray

before this relic and beg for the saint's help. The jewel is a courtly version of the mass-produced lead badges representing the saints, or their emblems, which were sold across Europe and worn as the proof of a successful pilgrimage. Sporting the shell emblem often worn by pilgrims, a jet figure of St James of Compostela is set in a silver frame with a loop at the back to secure it to a cap (**24**). Compostela, in northern Spain, was one of the principal European pilgrimage sites from the 12th to the 18th century.

Designs for men's hat jewels were often taken from the Old Testament, Greek and Roman mythology, or personal or emblematic devices. As the Florentine goldsmith Benvenuto Cellini explained: 'At this time you would use some small medals of gold, upon which each man or gentleman like to have engraved his whim or device and they would wear these on their hats.'[3] Men in contemporary paintings, such as an unknown man portrayed by Bartolomeo Veneto (**22**), wear jewelled and enamelled badges set in their caps. Archaeological evidence suggests that silver or copper-alloy hat jewels may also have been worn at lower levels of society.[4]

A circular jewel set with a ruby heart pierced with diamond arrows (**25**) was probably worn at court in Prague in the early 17th century. As now, the heart was indicative of romantic love, symbolized by Cupid's arrows striking the lover's heart. A small locket on the back of the jewel holds a later miniature painting of a man, suggesting that it was once a betrothal or wedding

22 *Portrait of a Gentleman*, by Bartolomeo Veneto, c.1512.
Galleria d'Arte Antica, Palazzo Barberini, Rome.
Photo: Araldo de Luca/Corbis via Getty Images

gift. In 1589, James VI of Scotland sent a similar jewel with a crowned amethyst heart to the 14-year-old Anne of Denmark as a token of their marriage, along with a poem likening his undying love to the heart-shaped jewel.[5] However, the heart was also the vital centre of the Galenic system of bodily humors, functioning as the source of heat, while humoral fluids directed health and emotion within the body. Equally, it was the centre of religious emotion and a window into the soul. Meditating on the sacred heart of Jesus was a means of accessing the divine source of redemption and everlasting love. In theologian Daniel Cramer's *Emblemata Sacra* (1624), the heart pierced by arrows has been pierced by God's love, to be reborn into eternal life.[6]

Particular gemstones held significance beyond gorgeous adornment, codified in written lapidaries based on the writings of Pliny the Elder, Aristotle and Dioscorides, as well as medieval authors such as Bishop Marbode of Rennes, Albertus Magnus and Bartholomeus Anglicus. Even if not universally credited, these texts influenced the way in which 16th- and 17th-century customers chose and wore jewellery. In the dialogue between the goldsmith and customer in Pierre Erondelle's *The French Garden* (1605), the diamond is described as that 'which is esteemed the chiefest of Stones and called the Stone of Love forasmuch as it has vertue to reconcile and renew (yea rather encrease) love in them that are married, being in discord, by a hidden vertue that nature (or to speak more properly God) hath given it to gain good affection in those that carie it'.[7] In a humorous note, he also explained: 'The precious stones, Madame, have many great properties. But that which is most profitable unto us, it is the force they have to transport the money from your purse into ours.' The diamond was also, according to the author of the *Pharmacopoeia Londinensis* (1691), the 'hardest of all gems.... So it's said to take away Fears, Melancholy and to strengthen the heart.'[8]

23 Gold and enamel, inscribed in Latin ('Among them that are born of women, there hath not risen one [greater than John the Baptist]'). France, c.1500–25.
473-1873

A breast ornament (**26**) was made in the *cosse de pois* or 'pea-pod style' that originated in Paris around 1615. The sculptural gold framework, set with 208 diamonds, created a splendid jewel, which also promoted marital harmony. These large, sparkling jewels were usually attached to the low neckline of dresses. Portraits, such as a painting of a young lady by Paulus Moreelse (**27**), show that they were sometimes set on rosettes of ribbon.

The closed settings used for diamonds gave diamond-set jewellery a darker glitter compared to modern jewels. The principal effect of diamonds before the development of the brilliant cut came from the light reflected from their surface due to their extremely bright lustre. Jewellers, such as the author of the late 17th-century Sloane manuscript, distinguished between a diamond that was of 'clear white perfection' or 'brite' and a diamond that was 'shining and clear but which has a yellow or blackish tint to it', which would fetch a far

smaller price.[9] However, the appearance and colour of unsatisfactory gems could be improved by painting the underside of the gem with a coloured tint or by setting it on a reflective or coloured metal foil. When diamonds were set on a black backing, the mirror-like flash of the lustre was greatly enhanced. Setting small gems in large metal collets would trick the eye into seeing a larger stone. The stone setter who worked on the pea-pod-style breast ornament (see **26**) drew the gold facets up to the widest edge of the diamonds to make the most of rather small, irregular stones.[10]

The supply of diamonds increased greatly with the discovery of important deposits in Brazil and the opening of the Minas Gerais mine in 1725, supplementing the traditional trade from India. The sudden influx of such large quantities of diamonds, according to the 1751 treatise of the jeweller David Jeffries, 'occasioned many, even of the most capital traders in London, to believe that Diamonds were likely to become

24 Jet and silver. Spain (Santiago de Compostela), c.1600–1700.
A.16-1953. Given by Dr W.L. Hildburgh

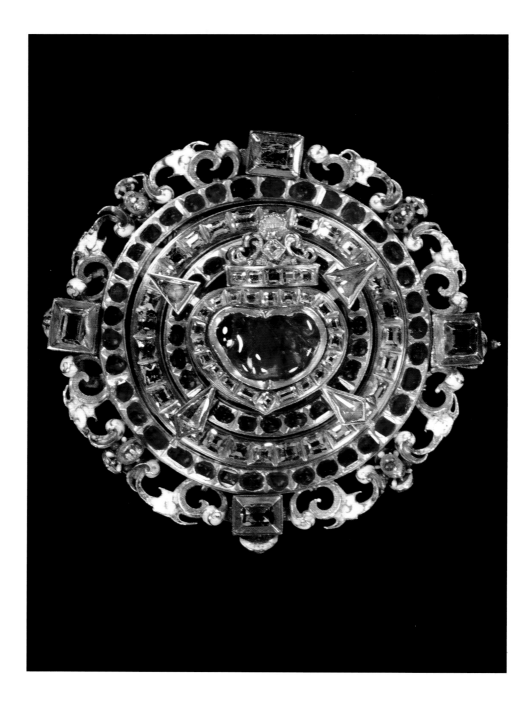

25 Gold, enamel, table-cut diamonds, rubies and emeralds.
Probably Prague, c.1610–20.
M.461-1936. Given by the Countess Harley Teleki

26 Gold, enamel and diamonds.
Possibly France, c.1620–30.
M.143-1975. Given by Dame Joan Evans

as plenty as transparent pebbles; and ... most of them refused to buy diamonds on any terms'.[11] Despite these anxieties, diamonds, either rose-cut or in the newer brilliant cut, remained in high esteem.

Chrysoberyls, pink topazes, garnets, rock crystal and glass pastes were a cheaper but attractive alternative to diamonds, rubies and emeralds. The intoxicating effect produced by sparkling jewels set on silk dresses was evocatively rendered in the *Spectator* in January 1712, in which theatre boxes filled with brightly dressed women were compared to 'Beds of Tulips': 'so great an Assembly of Ladies placed in gradual Rows in all the Ornaments of Jewels, Silks and Colours, gave so lively and gay an impression to the Heart, that methought the Season of the Year was vanished'.[12] The type of jewellery worn at this time depended on social status as much as the means of the wearer. David Jeffries expressed the generally held belief that these were essential items in

creating a splendid and appropriate appearance: 'persons of rank and fortune ... are the proper purchasers of jewels; and the money laid out by such persons can no more be deemed luxury in them than that which is expended in equipping and furnishing sideboards and cabinets, and on all other costly personal equipments in gold and silver'.[13]

Emeralds were as highly valued as diamonds for their limpid green colour and their supposed power to reveal truth and confound enchantments. The Spanish invasion of South America in the 16th century gave access to the fabulous emerald deposits of Colombia, and international trade from Cartagena allowed the stones to reach the European cities of Seville, Lisbon, Venice, Antwerp, Amsterdam and London.[14] One large gold and emerald breast ornament (**28**) is set with table-cut emeralds and smaller diamonds and fitted with a large hook on the back to slot into a rigid dress bodice. A print after David Baumann (**29**) shows a series

27 *Portrait of a Young Lady*, by Paulus Moreelse, c.1620.
Photo: The Art Institute of Chicago, IL, USA/Bridgeman Images

28 Enamelled gold, table-cut emeralds and diamonds. Spain, 1700–15.
325-1870

of brooches and breast ornaments in similar floral designs set with quantities of rose-cut gemstones.

The fashion for bow jewels developed in the first half of the 17th century, probably in the Low Countries. They were inspired by fabric bows that were attached to both male and female clothing, often with a precious stone set in the centre.[15] These cloth or ribbon bows developed into jewels set with pearls and gemstones, the backs often enamelled with floral patterns. In 1690, Antoine Furetière's *Dictionnaire universel* underlined their prevalence: 'women have had bows in their hair, bows on their sleeves, even bows of diamonds and precious stones in places where nothing but a simple clasp was needed'.[16] The varying sizes of three diamond bows (**30**) indicate that the larger bow was probably worn on the bodice, while the two smaller ones were worn on the shoulders. Surviving jewels in the Kremlin in Moscow suggest that they were originally fitted with vertical pins.[17]

The brilliant-cut stones allowed rays of light to be reflected through the pavilion facets of the diamonds and back through the crown to create rainbow flashes of colour. The diamonds are set in silver to offset the whiteness of the stone.

Popular literature provided the inspiration for a brooch set with a blue jasperware cameo in a polished cut-steel frame (**31**). The figure of the 'Bourbonnais Shepherd' was based on Laurence Sterne's *A Sentimental Journey through France and Italy*, first published in 1768, shortly before Sterne's death. Shepherds and shepherdesses were totems of a simple, picturesque life; Sterne had earlier dedicated his great novel *Tristram Shandy* (1759) to a notional shepherd sitting with his faithful dogs.

Josiah Wedgwood perfected the formula for jasperware in the late 1770s at the Etruria works in Stoke-on-Trent, producing finely modelled, pure white cameos on a tinted ground, which

29 Design from *Ein Neues Buch von allerhand Gold-Arbeit*, after David Baumann. Augsburg, 1695.
E.1069-1908.

30 Silver and brilliant-cut diamonds. Europe, c.1760.
M.93 and 94&A-1951. Cory Bequest

were set in brooches, rings, necklaces, shoe buckles and earrings. Many designs echoed fashionable Neoclassicism, but others depicted contemporary figures and political causes such as the campaign to abolish slavery. A number of cameo designs were created by Lady Templetown, who often began with a silhouette in 'beautiful cut Indian paper'.[18] Wedgwood jewellery was frequently set in cut-steel mounts made by friend and fellow Midlands entrepreneur Matthew Boulton. The glittering steel mounts and colourful cameo brooches were seen to good effect pinned on the neckline or shoulders of light-coloured, softly draped dresses and tunics 'à la Diane', inspired by classical statuary.

Hearts – single, twinned, flaming, crowned or pierced with arrows – remained a perennial symbol of love, and heart brooches were worn at all levels of society. Here, an 18th-century silver brooch from Scotland (**32**) is set with rock crystals and a garnet. The heart was also

believed to have amuletic power: a brooch given to the National Museum of Scotland in 1893 was 'worn on the breast of the chemise by the grandmother of the donor, to prevent the witches from taking away her milk'.[19] Children wore heart brooches pinned inside their petticoats to avert the evil eye and protect them from spirits.

A French brooch set with seed pearls and a pair of flaming, enamelled hearts is unmistakably a love jewel (**33**). Cupid's bow and arrows encircle a pair of doves, the bird of Venus, while a gold and pearl torch is a reference to Hymen, the Greek god of marriage. The brooch was made around 1800, just ten years after the upheavals of the French Revolution. The subject is light-hearted and hints at the return of confidence under the First Consul Napoleon Bonaparte, which led to the public flocking to the theatres, costume balls and other public entertainments. Demand for fashionable dress and jewellery rose accordingly, heralding the start of the new century.

31 Cut and polished steel, blue jasper-dip with white cameo. Possibly designed by Lady Templetown, made by Josiah Wedgwood and Sons Ltd. Etruria, England, c.1780–1800. 414:1286-1885. Given by Lady Charlotte Schreiber

32 Silver, rock crystals and garnet. Scotland, 1700–1800.
M.76-1962. Given by Dame Joan Evans

33 Gold, enamel, cornelians, pearls and emeralds. France, c.1800.
M.37-1962. Given by Dame Joan Evans

CHAPTER THREE

'Any number of brooches, up and down and everywhere'
1800–1900

The 19th century was the prime age of the brooch, worn by women and men in an endless variety of styles, materials and sizes. Elizabeth Gaskell's mid-century novel, *Cranford*, gives a vivid, fondly mocking impression of the ladies of the town wearing 'any number of brooches, up and down and everywhere (some with dogs' eyes painted in them; some that were like small picture frames with mausoleums and weeping willows neatly executed in hair inside; some, again, with miniatures of ladies and gentlemen sweetly smiling out of a nest of stiff muslin)'.[1]

Women's fashions provided many opportunities for wearing brooches. In the day, dress fronts or blouses were trimmed with ribbons and falls of lace held in order by small decorative brooches, whether plain or in whimsical, humorous designs reflecting the wearer's interests. From the 1850s to the early 1900s, large brooches were pinned to the high necklines of dresses. The low bodices of evening dresses were decorated with gem-set brooches.

The fashion for cameo brooches began at the French court early in the century, stimulated by Napoleon's Italian campaign in 1796. By the 1840s, large cameo brooches were worn at the neck, on the breast, pinning ribbons or looping up the 'drapery of ... lace sleeves'.[2] When Maria Dominica Ricci was painted in 1854, she wore a large cameo brooch pinned on a pink rosette at the neck of her jacket (**34**).

Visiting Italian cameo and mosaic workshops was an essential part of the European travels of the well-educated middle and upper classes. In 1840, Catherine Taylor described visiting workshops in Rome and seeing the manufacture of cameos from 'helmet shell, which has many coats of different thickness and colour. By skillfully removing these, the figures are left in fine relief of white on a gray or sometimes red ground. I have been much interested in watching Saulini, one of the best artists of his profession, engaged at his work, as he gently cut away the superfluous shell and revealed the figure. The instruments he employs are very minute and sharp and the workmanship is so delicate that it requires a steady and skilful hand.'[3]

Brooches set with mosaics and cameos formed delightful souvenirs or made gifts for those at home: the shell allowed a large image to be produced, while still being light enough to make a wearable piece of jewellery. Subjects were 'generally chosen from antique gems or statues, sometimes from celebrated pictures, and frequently from the works of modern sculptors'.[4] Personal portraits were also a popular choice.

The appreciation of cameos depended on a shared visual language: wearing an image taken from art or literature marked the wearer as educated and well travelled. The cameo of the sprite Ariel riding on the back of a bat (**35**) was based on a contemporary painting by Joseph Severn, inspired by Shakespeare's last play, *The Tempest*. Shakespeare was hailed as England's bard, and his plays were widely available through illustrated editions.[5] The cameo

34 *Maria Dominica Ricci*, by Emma Ekwall, 1854.
Photo: Erik Cornelius/Nationalmuseum Stockholm

35 Gold and shell, probably by the studio of Tommaso Saulini.
England and Italy, c.1840.
M.274-1921. Given by Mrs L.M. Festing

36 Shell, gold, emeralds and diamonds, carved by Paul Victor Lebas
and mounted by Félix Dafrique. France, 1851.
M.340-1977

may have been made in Tommaso Saulini's Rome workshop. Severn painted *Ariel* while living in Rome and it is possible that Saulini negotiated directly with Severn, as he is known to have done with landscape painter Thomas Cole.[6]

Cameo carving was also used for portraiture, creating official portraits such as French carver Paul Victor Lebas's likeness of Queen Victoria (**36**) for the firm of Dafrique. They won a medal at the 1851 Great Exhibition for their 'polychromatic cameos, with metal and enamel ornaments, a happy invention, well carried out'[7] – a group which probably included this brooch. The image is based on the 1838 painting of Queen Victoria by the American artist Thomas Sully, though small differences in the cameo indicate that it was probably copied from an 1839 engraving by Henri Grevedon rather than from the original work.

While shell cameos could be finished in a matter of days, allowing travellers to commission portraits and personal designs, mosaic brooches were far more time-consuming and more expensive. Brightly coloured images were formed by piecing together tiny pieces of glass

paste, or *smalti*, which were manufactured 'in the shape of crayons, or little sticks of sealing wax and are afterwards drawn out by the workman at a blow-pipe to the thickness he requires, often almost to a hair, and now seldom thicker than the finest grass-stalk'.[8]

These brooches were decorated with birds, flowers and scenes inspired by Roman art or classical temples, and were bought as travel souvenirs. 'The beauty of the workmanship, the soft gradation of the tints, and the cost depend on the minuteness of the pieces and the skill displayed by the artist. A ruin, a group of flowers or figures will employ a good artist about two months when only two inches square, and a specimen of such a description costs from five pounds to twenty pounds.'[9]

A brooch set with red and blue mosaics is decorated with a cherub's head, alongside Christian imagery and the inscription 'Roma' (**37**). An erupting volcano in the bottom panel may refer to Vesuvius and the buried city of Pompeii, which was rediscovered in 1748, bringing long-lost Roman art and jewellery back into view. The brooch was made as part of a parure with a matching necklace, bracelet and ring.

37 Gold and glass micromosaic. Italy, c.1870.
LOAN:GILBERT.128-2008. The Rosalinde and Arthur Gilbert Collection
on loan to the Victoria and Albert Museum, London

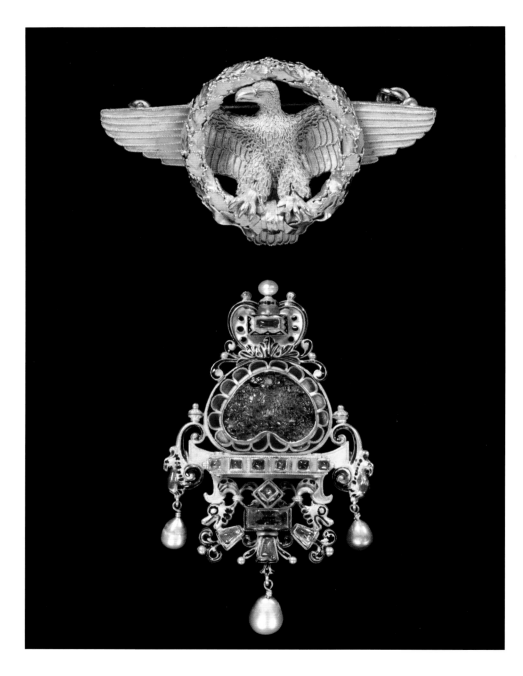

38 Gold, by Castellani. Italy, c.1860.
M.11-2011. Given by the American Friends of the V&A through the generosity of Judith H. Siegel

39 Enamelled gold, pearls, rubies, diamond and a sapphire intaglio.
Intaglio by Giorgio Antonio Girardet, brooch by Augusto Castellani. Italy, 1887–8.
M.222-1917. Bequeathed by Henry L. Florence

Jewels by the Castellani family and other makers were fashionable among followers of the Pre-Raphaelite movement, such as the poet Elizabeth Barrett Browning and Fanny, the wife of painter William Holman Hunt. A gold brooch shaped as a Roman Imperial eagle was shown at London's 1862 International Exhibition and illustrated in the exhibition reports (**38**). Castellani's display was received with such great acclaim that a special policeman had to be deployed to contain the public's enthusiasm.[10]

Although Castellani's Renaissance-style jewellery did not meet with the same immediate praise as the classically inspired pieces, the firm's research into enamelling was an important stage in the renewal of the art. One brooch (**39**) was inspired by a Renaissance design but commemorates a contemporary political event: the massacre by the Ethiopian army of an Italian invasion force in 1887. The battle scene engraved with minute detail on the sapphire (**40**) was taken from a print published in *L'Illustrazione italiana*.[11]

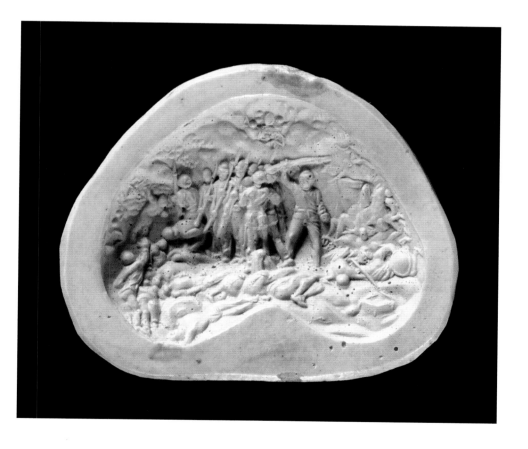

40 Cast of engraved sapphire from pendant brooch by Augusto Castellani (**39**).
M.222-1917

41 Silver-gilt and coral, by James West and Son. Ireland, c.1850.
2750-1853

42 Gold, bloodstone, red jasper and agate, by G. & M. Crichton.
Edinburgh, Scotland, c.1880.
M.55-1980

Over in Ireland, in the late 18th and early 19th century, archaeological excavations had uncovered spectacular hoards of Bronze Age and early Christian objects. In the mid-1840s, the Irish Academy of Arts allowed Dublin jewellers such as George Waterhouse and Company and West and Son to study and make copies of the objects in its collection. A silver-gilt and coral brooch, by West and Son (**41**), was a small-scale adaptation of the Cavan brooch, a Celtic brooch from the late 8th century, now in the National Museum of Ireland.

In the early years of the 19th century, the poetry and novels of Sir Walter Scott put Scotland on the tourist map. Royal favour confirmed this when Queen Victoria and Prince Albert built Balmoral Castle as a holiday home. Scottish pebble jewellery, already fashionable in the 18th century, became a popular souvenir. 'Rough and valueless as many of these gems appear when found on the mountainside, in the river bed or on the sea-shore, their beauties shine out pleasantly when cut by the lapidary and polished by his wheels and diamond dust and arranged in order of their colours and set in gold or silver', claimed the *Jeweller and Fancy Trades Advertiser* in 1868.[12] A brooch by Edinburgh jewellers G. & M. Crichton (**42**) was set with jasper and bloodstone in a vaguely Celtic design. Birmingham jewellers followed the trend, though some of their jewellery evokes a Scottish association only through the use of the stone settings or 'pebbles'. The design for one 'Scottish pebble' brooch (**43**) was registered by the Birmingham firm of James Fenton on 14 October 1865.

Acceptable men's jewellery at the beginning of the 19th century included brooches, stick and tie pins, signet rings, watches and chains worn with typically plain but neatly tailored clothing. Carefully tied cravats or stocks were added to white linen shirts and decorated with gold,

43 Silver and granite ('Scottish pebbles'), by James Fenton.
Birmingham, England, c.1865.
CIRC.278-1961

44 *Midshipman Robert Deans*, British School, c.1807.
Photo © National Maritime Museum, Greenwich, London

pearl or diamond brooches. A portrait of Midshipman Robert Deans shows the pleated frill of his shirt pinned with a gold and paste or diamond brooch (**44**). Hints of this can be found in contemporary crime reports: in 1815, London jeweller George Bannister, accosted by two women who put their hands around his neck, complained that 'I perceived my shirt frill out, and on putting my hand up, found my brooch gone'.[13] By the middle of the century, however, this type of brooch was so out of favour that *Cranford*'s Miss Matty could refer to the 'strange, uncouth brooch with which her father had disfigured his shirt-frill'.[14]

Jane Carlyle's description of the fashionable dandy, the Count d'Orsay, in 1840, draws attention to his 'two glorious breast pins, attached by a chain', which by 1845 had declined somewhat to a single breast pin: 'a large pear-shaped pearl set in a little cup of diamonds'.[15] Pins provided a chance for imagination and daring in men's jewellery. The tops of the pins were set with gemstones or less precious stones, or shaped to reflect the wearer's interests. A sheet of designs from the London firm of John Brogden shows a group of pins aimed at the horseman or racing enthusiast (**45**).

A stick pin topped with a skull was an object intended to startle and amuse (**46**). Jeweller Auguste-Germain Cadet-Picard made these 'electro-mobile' jewels for the inventor Gustave Trouvé, the creator of the 'Lilliputian battery' that enabled the pieces to make a sensation at the Hotel Continental in Paris in 1879. A writer from *La Nature* described the effect they made: 'Some of the guests are wearing Trouvé's charming electric jewels: a death's head tie-pin; a rabbit drummer tie-pin. Suppose you are carrying one of these jewels below your chin. Whenever someone takes a look at it, you discreetly slip your hand into the pocket of your waistcoat, tip the tiny battery to horizontal and immediately the death's head rolls its glittering eyes and grinds its teeth. The rabbit starts working like the timpanist at the opera.'[16]

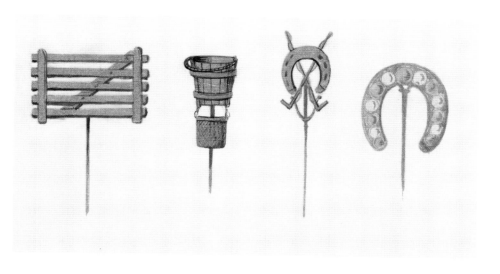

45 Designs for jewellery, by the firm of John Brogden. London, England, c.1860.
E.2:821-1986

At the end of the century, some men used brooches to pin a sash around their waists, although this was not universally approved. The Duc de Morny appeared at the fashionable seaside resort of Deauville in 1893, resplendent in a shot taffeta crimson and pink cummerbund fastened by 'two brooches of large pink pearls surrounded by diamonds'. However, 'imagine that abomination of desolation, the cheap swell, aping all the splendor with cheap silks, brass buckles and imitation jewellery', wrote a disdainful *Vogue* reporter, 'and you will understand why our gilded youth have been compelled to abandon the cummerbund.'[17]

A layered agate brooch by the Franco-German artist Jean Georges Bissinger suited less flamboyant tastes (**47**). The finely carved agate shows Bissinger's father-in-law, Carl Rudolf Brunnarius, a publisher and merchant. He is conventionally dressed, and is himself depicted wearing a brooch set with a cameo of a man pinned beneath his shirt collar. The journal *Public Opinion* admired Bissinger's work, which was often small-scale and in the antique style, and lamented the decline in popularity for hardstone cameos, feeling that 'if our millionaires would only realize that their portraits cut on onyx would be infinitely more permanent than if painted in oils, sculptured in marble, or figured in bronze, they would find that artists exist who are capable of producing such work in great perfection'.[18]

Jewellery inspired by and, in many cases, actually made from, birds, beetles and other insects was wildly popular in the late 19th century. Brazil, which had thousands of varieties of brilliantly coloured native beetles, was a common source of raw materials. Some jewels were set with whole beetles; others used their shells to create a decorative scheme. A short-lived

46 (left) Gold, enamel and diamond, by Auguste-Germain Cadet-Picard. France, c.1867.
M.121-1984

47 (right) Gold and layered agate, by Jean Georges Bissinger. France, c.1872.
M.12-2018. Given by Christine Wishart

fashion even saw some women wearing a live beetle on a tiny gold chain pinned to their dress. The iridescent colours of various birds and beetles were particularly highly prized. Though fashion gradually moved away from the use of the actual beetle, brooches were still set with realistic insects (**48**).

Marrying couples were expected to give gifts to their bridesmaids and ushers, most commonly brooches or lockets for the women and stick pins for the men. A brooch by the architect and designer William Burges was made as a bridesmaid's gift for the 1864 wedding of fellow architect John Pollard Seddon to Margaret Barber (**49**). The design was inspired by medieval jewellery, while the turquoise-set flowers and garnet heart symbolized love. A drawing of the brooch, marked 'Seddon', survives in an album of designs (**50**). Bridesmaids' brooches were often linked to the lives of the

couples. When Mary Oliphant Wilson married Captain Fitzherbert in 1895, the dragon brooch she wore and the jewelled dragon pins given to her bridesmaids referred to the unofficial crest of her husband's regiment.[19] An autumn wedding in 1896 was celebrated with 'the bridegroom's gift brooches of diamond Michaelmas geese in honor of the wedding day',[20] and another with flag-shaped 'burgee brooches with the name of [the groom's] yacht in emeralds on the white enamel'.[21] A point of confusion in transatlantic society weddings was that British grooms expected to provide the gift for the bridesmaids, while in America this was the responsibility of the bride.

The choice of design, colour and materials in jewels all carried meanings, reinforced by popular literature, fashion magazines, art, and books on the language of flowers and gemstones. A hand holding a vine symbolized

48 Gold, enamel and diamond. Probably England, c.1880.
M.62-2003. Given by Roger and Geoffrey Munn in memory of their parents

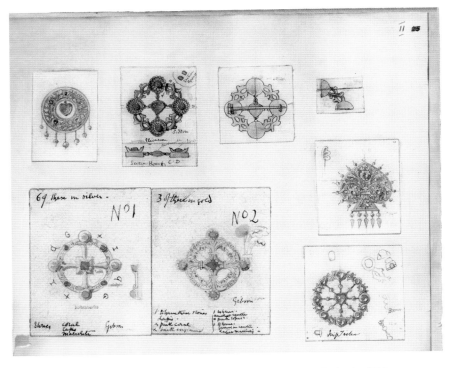

49 Silver, silver-gilt, turquoise and garnet, by William Burges. England, c.1864.
M.8-2012. Given by William and Judith Bollinger

50 Designs for brooches, in pen, pencil, and watercolour, by William Burges.
England, c.1855–81.
8830:11

51 Gold, silver, diamond and enamel. Probably UK or USA, 1880–1900.
M.1-2014. Given by Geoffrey and Caroline Munn

52 Enamelled gold, turquoise, coral, pearls and ruby, designed by Sir Edward Burne-Jones
and made by Carlo Giuliano. London, c.1885–95.
M.11-2015. Given by Geoffrey and Caroline Munn through the Art Fund

53 Gold, the back inscribed 'Sir Marc Isambard Brunel died Decr 1849. Aged 80.
Sophia Brunel, Died Jany 1855, Aged 79'. England, 1855.
M.21-1972. Given by Miss A. Kelsey

54 Carved jet. England (probably North Yorkshire), c.1870.
M.944D-1983

fruitfulness; and a blue flower, possibly a forget-me-not, true love (**51**). A spirited turquoise and coral bird brooch is a version of the brooch first designed by the artist Sir Edward Burne-Jones as a gift for his daughter Margaret, possibly inspired by a plate in John Ruskin's *Stones of Venice* (**52**).

Hair was a uniquely evocative item, cut from both the living and the dead. Friends and lovers exchanged locks of hair, and mourners agreed that it was 'the most lasting and delicate of our memorials, and survives us like love'.[22] The inscription on the back of one brooch (**53**) tells us that the mingled locks belonged to engineer Sir Marc Isambard Brunel and his wife Sophia. Locks of hair from the famous were also sought by celebrity hunters and collectors as secular relics.

The premature death of Prince Albert propelled Queen Victoria into an extreme and prolonged period of mourning. Society rules on mourning, especially for women, were strict. Jewellery, apart from wedding rings, was required to be of plain matt black jet or black enamel, although pearls were permissible in the later

stages. Jet, a fossilized wood found principally around Whitby in North Yorkshire, became the basis of fashionable jewels. It was dense and easy to carve, but light enough for wear. Jewels were often made with mass-produced lathe-turned bases, to which hand-carved detail was added, bringing the cost down and making them more widely available. One brooch (**54**), set with a medallion of 'Night', was worn with a matching necklace, bracelet and earrings.

Mass production in Birmingham in England, in Newark, New Jersey and Providence, Rhode Island in America, and the huge industry of Germany's Pforzheim makers brought brooches to people at all income levels. A demonstration model from the 1872 Exhibition in London (**55**) by the Birmingham firm of T. & J. Bragg shows how a simple gold brooch could be created from a dozen machine-stamped gold parts. Factory-produced jewellery in gilt metal, sometimes set with imitation stones, responded to rapidly changing fashions. However, this democratization of jewellery design was seen as a threat by some beholders. A correspondent to the *Ladies Home Journal* of 1892 bemoaned the way in which 'cheap jewelry masquerading

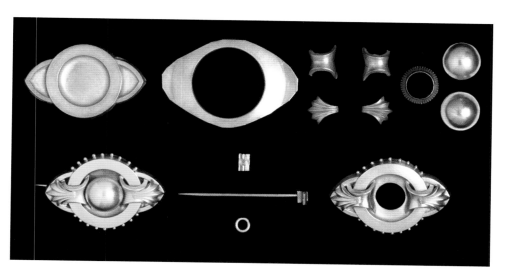

55 Machine-made gold brooch and die-stamped component parts, by T. & J. Bragg. Birmingham, England, 1872.
915:1, 2, A to M-1875

in the guise of real; the thousand and one bow-knots and Rhine-stone pins; and fake enamel trinkets that now glitter in the shop-windows – and their adoption by maidservants and shop-girls – are no doubt responsible for the forsaking of much that is fascinating and appropriate for wear in the goldsmiths art'.[23]

Gilt and electroplated brooches reflected contemporary politics, hobbies and sports. One brooch was aimed at supporters of the British Liberal prime minister, William Gladstone, who made his hobby of tree husbandry a key part of his public image (**56**). Meanwhile, an electroplated brooch in the shape of a tennis racquet and ball (**57**) spoke to the stylish game of outdoor tennis, newly accessible to women barred from male-only indoor courts. This brooch might have been worn on a fashionable, tight-fitting dress while playing, or on a day

dress, to show that the wearer was a modern, active woman.

Brightly coloured and three-dimensional images were created by engraving and then painting a design with very fine brushes on the reverse of a polished rock crystal half-dome. A range of sentimental and fashionable images were featured, such as 'a portrait, the head of a dog, of a fox, a hearse, or a flower, or a monogram or a crest, indeed any suitable subject ... the crystal set as a brooch, the centre of a bracelet, a breast pin or a ring as the case may be'.[24] The little dog with a blue ribbon bow (**58**) appears to be a Yorkshire terrier, a breed that was developed in the mid-19th century. Another brooch (**59**) is set with a crystal painted with a sailor's straw 'sennit' hat tied with a ribbon bearing the name of the ship HMS *Minotaur*. Jewels relating to particular ships may have been worn

56 (left) Silver-gilt. Birmingham, England, 1898–9.
M.33-1977. Given by Mrs John Hull Grundy
57 (right) Electroplated nickel silver. England, c.1880.
M.23-1977. Given by Mrs John Hull Grundy

58 Gold and reverse intaglio crystal. England, c.1875–90.
M.65-1951. Cory Bequest
59 Gold and reverse intaglio crystal. England, c.1900–10.
M.71-1979. Given by Miss Crawford

60 Platinum, gold, diamonds, ruby, natural pearl and emerald,
by Marcus & Co. New York, 1875–1900.
M.146-2007. Given by the American Friends of the V&A
through the generosity of Patricia V. Goldstein

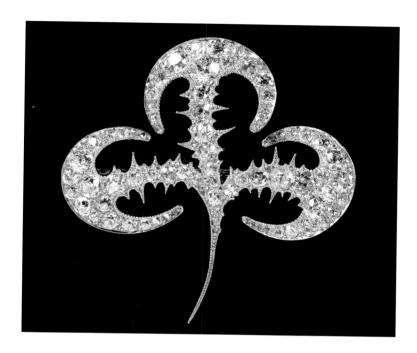

by the wives, mothers or girlfriends of serving sailors. Nautical styles were also more widely fashionable, especially for children.

Butterflies were another popular motif. The butterfly was traditionally associated with transience and the rebirth of the soul, and it could also be a symbol of romance. It fitted well with the collection of jewelled bats, spiders and insects that bedecked contemporary women's dresses (**60**).

Evening dress required a profusion of sparkling jewels. Brooches were pinned to the bodice or set on the shoulder. The 'quite modern custom of fastening down the waistband with costly ornaments at the back' was warned against, for 'many greedy eyes are fixed upon the diamond and emerald lizards or single stone mounted gold safety pins which are so much worn at weddings, garden parties or other outdoor functions'.[25] In the last years of the century, brooches were put to use to pin the loose hairs at the back of the head.

Diamonds were generally considered suitable only in the evening or at formal functions. They were used to create the three-leaved brooch designed by René Lalique for Tiffany & Co (**61**). The crescent moon, associated with the goddess Diana, was also a popular design (**62, 63**). The renewed taste for diamonds did not meet approval in every quarter and the French jeweller Lucien Falize regretted the fashion for lavish jewels. 'The precious stone', he felt, 'is not enhanced by a sophisticated design, it defies all forms of embellishment. Its fires sparkle with geometric shadow and light, interfering with every conceivable type of decoration. Elegant modelling, finely chased detail and depths of ornamentation are lost as in a gigantic firework display in which the architect's designs have vanished, leaving only dazzling light and wonderment.'[26]

61 Platinum, gold and diamonds, designed by René Lalique for Tiffany & Co. Paris, c.1895.
M.140-2007. Given by the American Friends of the V&A through the generosity of Patricia V. Goldstein

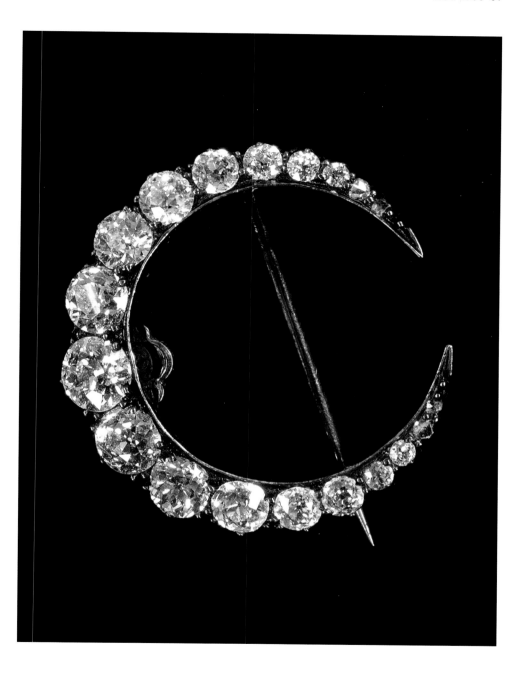

62 *Invitation to the Waltz*, by Francesco Miralles Galaup, 1895.
Circulo del Liceo, Barcelona, Spain.
Photo: Heritage Image Partnership Ltd/Alamy Stock Photo

63 Gold and brilliant-cut diamonds. England, c.1890s.
M.98-1978. Bequeathed by Mrs D.B. Simpson

CHAPTER FOUR

'The new jewel has been born'
1900–1920

In 1898, Henri Vever published a rallying cry directed at his fellow jewellers:

We have been as if hypnotised by the past for too long, stubbornly borrowing our decorative motifs from doubtless very venerable, consecrated motifs, but which are nowadays powerless and sterile; too long we have exhausted ourselves walking in the tracks of our forebears, without trying to explore new paths, and in this torpor, we risked forfeiting our inventive faculties forever.[1]

The turn of the 20th century saw the popularity of jewels inspired by historical tradition challenged by the explosive advent of Art Nouveau. René Lalique's jewellery caused a sensation in Paris at the 1900 Exposition Universelle, crowds swarming to see his shocking and innovative jewels.[2] French jeweller Alphonse Fouquet's judgment of Lalique's work when shown earlier, in 1884, was shared by many tired of the more conventional products of the jewellery houses: 'I was not aware of the existence of any contemporary jewellery designers, and at last, here is one!'[3] Lalique's work was characterized by a careful and serious observation of nature, resulting in designs that were based on every stage in a plant's life cycle but also employing the fantastical imagery of Art Nouveau. He combined gemstones and precious metals with less traditional materials, such as horn or glass, which could be coloured and formed at will.[4] One bodice ornament is set with curves of enamelled gold, supporting a group of delicately translucent sweet-pea flowers (**66**). Another, set with a large aquamarine, uses glass coloured to a wintry blue to create two

thistles set in a spiky, diamond-studded framework (**67**). As with the earlier Arts and Crafts movement, Art Nouveau jewellery turned away from a preoccupation with valuable gemstones in favour of artistic expression, with the claim that 'Art will therefore … take its revenge on the vanity of capital'.[5]

Wearing some Art Nouveau brooches demanded a degree of courage from women. As French magazine *Art et Décoration* pointed out, Lalique's popularity with actresses and artists did not make his jewels universally wearable: 'We are not all Sarah Bernhardt or Cléo de Mérode and a number of his pretty admirers are a little frightened by the originality he personifies, and which sometimes skirts eccentricity.'[6] The most daring excesses of Art Nouveau, however, were short-lived: by 1906, magazines were rejoicing over the abandonment of spiders, or the 'octopus whose tentacles of fine gemstones or enamel threatened to damage the flesh of the beautiful and adventurous persons who dared to adorn themselves with them'.[7] The new jewels were noted for the delicacy of their shapes and the ingenuity of their subject matter: 'The new jewel has been born, it is made for our time, it has abandoned its fossilized forms.'[8]

Two brooches by Georges Fouquet, inspired by plants, offered a modern but wearable version of Art Nouveau. The first is formed of a plaque with female busts worked in relief in gold, overlaid with coloured gold mistletoe leaves set with pearl berries, with a fine, ribbon-like border of diamonds (**68**). Fouquet began making Art Nouveau jewellery in 1898 and had a close

64 Colour lithograph poster, by Alphonse Mucha. France, 1897.
E.583-1953. Given by Mrs F.W. Templeton. © ADAGP, Paris, and DACS, London 1997

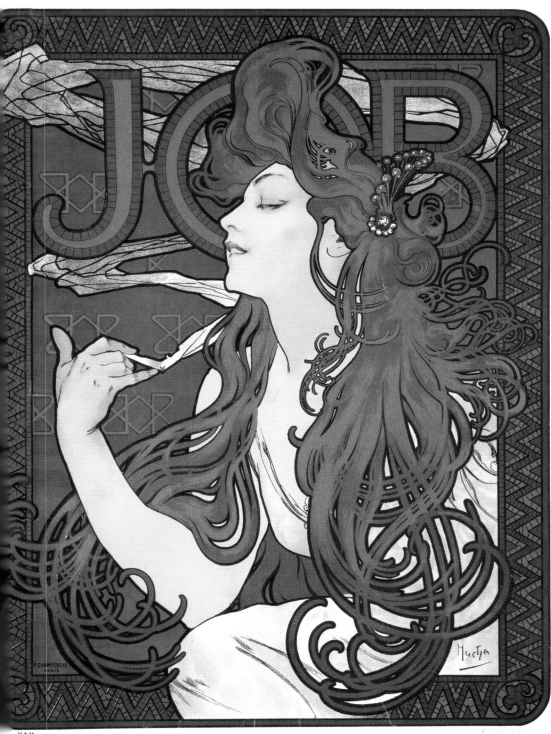

JOB

F. CHAMPENOIS
PARIS

Mucha

collaboration with the graphic artist Alphonse Mucha (**64**), an influence which may perhaps be seen in the female forms on the brooch. In 1902, Mucha published his *Documents Décoratifs*, a set of designs that included careful and realistic drawings of plants (**65**), the preface explaining that 'Mucha never tortures the flower through stylization; he loves it too much to harm it'.[9] Plants were valued not only as design motifs but also for their poetic and historic associations. In French folklore, mistletoe was associated with the Druids, who were said to cut it from sacred trees at the New Year, and it became a sign of prosperity for the coming year. The second brooch, designed by Charles Desrosiers, is a zigzag of bluish-green

enamel terminating in a flower head from which a hornet sips (**69**). Insects were a source of inspiration for many jewellers, sometimes disturbingly morphing into female forms, but here presented in a naturalistic fashion.

'It is noticeable too', reported *Vogue* magazine, 'that serpentine lines, vertical or horizontal, signify what is in design really chic.'[10] A gold brooch featuring curving lines set with bright green demantoid garnets (**70**) was at the forefront of American jewellery fashion. American customers particularly appreciated gemstones found in the USA, such as tourmalines, Montana sapphires, turquoise and Mississippi pearls.

65 Drawings of honesty, lily of the valley and mimosa, by Alphonse Mucha. Paris, 1902–3.
E.127-1964. Given by Mr Jirí Mucha, son of the Artist

66 Cast glass, enamelled gold and fire opal, by René Lalique. Paris, 1903–4.
M.116A-1966

67 Glass, gold, aquamarine and diamonds, by René Lalique. Paris, c.1905.
LOAN: MET ANON 10:1-2007. Lent through the generosity of
William & Judith, and Douglas and James Bollinger

68 Gold, silver, enamel, rose- and brilliant-cut diamonds, and pearls,
by Georges Fouquet. Paris, c.1903.

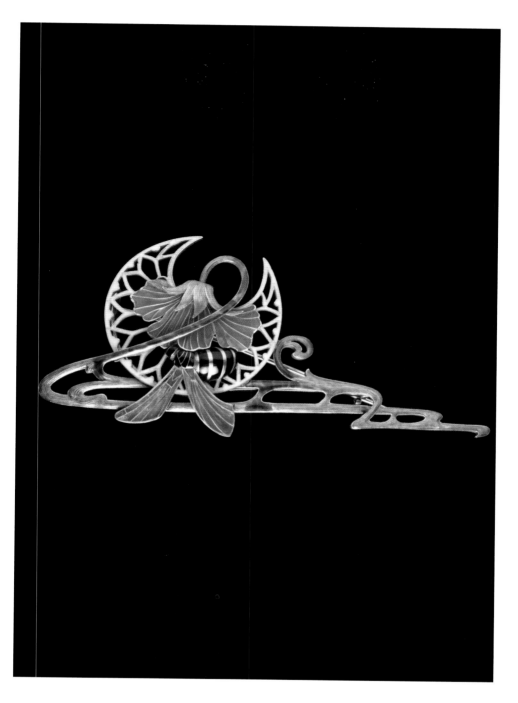

69 Gold and enamel, made by Georges Fouquet and designed
by Charles Desrosiers. Paris, 1901.

70 Gold, freshwater pearls, diamonds and demantoid garnets.
USA, c.1900.
M.207-2007. Given by the American Friends of the V&A
through the generosity of Patricia V. Goldstein

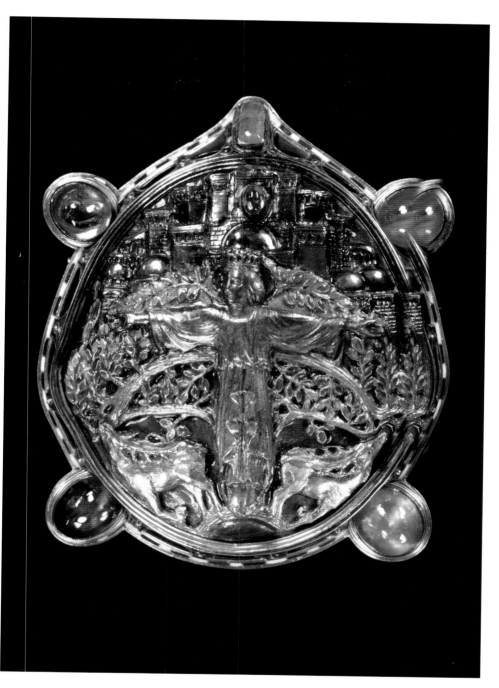

71 Enamelled gold, silver, pink sapphires and emerald,
by Henry Wilson. England, c.1906.
M.73-1979. Bought with the assistance of Thomas Stainton
in memory of Charles and Lavinia Handley-Read

Although Art Nouveau jewellery was sold by Liberty's department store to fashionable and forward-thinking British customers, jewels in the Arts and Crafts tradition continued to be favoured, sometimes to the puzzlement of Continental connoisseurs. The display of British Arts and Crafts jewellery in Paris at the Pavillon de Marsan in 1913 was generally positively received, though with some polite reservations: 'We remain a little surprised by these jewels, doubtless very appropriate for the English woman, but the French woman would adapt herself to them with difficulty.'[11]

Stones such as opals, moonstones, turquoise and citrines were widely used, chosen for the appeal of their colours rather than their intrinsic value. In an interview with *House Beautiful*'s art critic, American jeweller Elinor Klapp decried the reliance on traditional gemstones: 'I abominate diamonds … or rather I begrudge them their excessive prominence…'. In her view, the massing of brilliants was nothing more than 'a vulgar display of ill-used riches – it actually nullifies the special quality of the stone'.[12] The art of enamelling, widely exploited in the second half of the 19th century, brought brilliance and interest to jewels both in the Arts and Crafts and Art Nouveau traditions. Inspiration came from medieval and Renaissance jewels, as well as Japanese cloisonné enamels which were being imported into Europe from the 1850s onwards.

Henry Wilson was a master of enamelling and strongly inspired by medieval ornament. In the centre of his large pendant brooch (**71**), an embossed relief shows the crucified Christ against a leafy tree, with the Heavenly City in the background. Polished purplish star sapphires give the jewel an episcopal air. A brooch in the form of an enamelled Tudor rose was a gift from Wilson's brother Edgar to Alice Cooper, his new mother-in-law at the time of his wedding to Winifred Cooper in Tehran, December 1912 (**72**).

72 Enamelled gold, opals, moonstones and rock crystal, by Henry Wilson. England, c.1912.
M.13:1-2014. Given by John and Jim Howden and Marion Gladwell
in memory of Isobel Howden (née Wilson)

'Hats, gowns, cloaks, jewelry, household decorations, are all being affected by the peacock fad', noted the *Buffalo Tribune* in 1905. '[W]hen the peacock comes into fashion it gets into every phase of it...'.[13] Peacocks were staples of both Art Nouveau and Arts and Crafts jewellery. They were a traditional symbol of the Resurrection, but also symbolized pride and vanity. They were valued by designers for their gorgeous colouring and the artistic canvas offered by their fan-shaped tails. C.R. Ashbee's peacock brooch uses the shape of the peacock's tail feathers but in a soft, subtle combination of gold, silver and blister pearls (**73**). It was made as a gift for his wife Janet after their marriage in 1898. In a letter of March 1900, Ashbee wrote with news of the gift: 'Your peacock is finished. He is at the present moment pinned on my coat and is preening his tail and looking at himself with his ruby eye.'[14] It must have been the same brooch that Janet wore the following year on a tour of America to set up lectures

for Ashbee when she attended a '"grand dîner" at Mrs Hobson's, *decolleté*, peacock and all!!! ... I'm having a rare time.'[15]

Many jewellers continued to take inspiration from earlier styles. The artist and jeweller Reginald Pearson was described as 'deeply interested in "craftsmanship"' and investigated 'the methods, processes and technique of his favourite Old Masters' with his friend, sculptor Sidney Langford Jones.[16] He used engraved niello decoration and softly polished gemstones to create a brooch in the medieval taste for Arthur Morley Jones, Sidney's brother (**74**). The brooch, a necklace and an engagement ring were probably all made for Jones's fiancée Mary Houseman. This brooch, created around 1912 on the eve of the First World War, is a poignant reminder of their friendship. Pearson signed up to serve with the Artists' Rifles and was reported missing, presumed killed, in June 1915, just two months after Jones's wedding.

73 Silver, gold, blister pearl, garnet and brilliant-cut diamond, designed by C.R. Ashbee and made by the Guild of Handicraft. London, c.1900. M.31-2005. Accepted by HM Government in Lieu of Inheritance Tax and allocated to the Victoria and Albert Museum, 2005

74 (left) Gold, sapphire and moonstones, by Reginald Pearson. England, c.1912.
M.30-1995. Given by Katherine Chapman

75 (right) Partly gilded silver, abalone, turquoise, jade and citrine,
by Mary Thew. Scotland, c.1910–40.
M.12-2012. Given by Gulderen Tekvar

76 Gold, silver and enamel. UK, c.1900–10.
M.14:1-2002. Given by Helen Earle

The amateur and self-taught tradition of Arts and Crafts jewellery was friendly to female jewellers. Rather than training through craft apprenticeships, largely closed to women, they could study at art colleges and evening schools. As Delia Austrian explained in 1906, 'a woman who would make the new art jewellery must have a knowledge of design ... then a practical acquaintance with the practical side of working gold and silver and setting gems.... With a little lamp and blowpipe, a couple of hammers, some files and a few simple and inexpensive tools – adding perhaps a small forge and vise – many women have persevered with their trials until they have attained a degree of skill which entitles them to rank as experts.'[17] Jewellery making could give women an outlet for artistic expression and, just as importantly, the chance of financial independence. The involvement of women in the traditionally male field of jewellery manufacture echoes the demands for greater participation in public life exemplified by the suffrage movement.

Scottish jeweller Mary Thew turned to jewellery to support herself when she became a young widow. After only four jewellery classes she began to create jewels that united a mix of colourful stones with freely worked silver wire. Her brooch set with abalone, turquoise, jade and citrine is a careful balance of green and brown shades (**75**).

'Doesn't even the man most averse to jewellery wear a watch, a ring, a tie pin?' asked *Art et Décoration* magazine.[18] Tie pins and scarf pins were among the few acceptable items of jewellery for men at the beginning of the 20th century. Large diamonds were not generally approved of, but single pearls, gold crescents studded with small diamonds or single gemstones were acceptable. By 1900 *Vogue*'s views on pins reflecting sporting interests were firm – 'horseshoes, horse's heads, coaching horns, golf sticks and similar designs usually look just a little vulgar'[19] – but men often chose pins that indicated their interests. A small pin in the shape of a rapier overlaid with an enamelled Tudor rose (**76**) was formerly owned by Captain Alfred Hutton. Described as the 'most skillful swordsman in the Army',[20] Hutton revived the art of historical fencing in Britain.

77 Brass and enamel. UK, c.1909.
S.286-1984. Given by the British Theatre Museum Association

Unisex jewellery could also be presented as a keepsake of an event. A modest little brooch set with an enamelled bluebird was made as a souvenir for the London premiere of Maurice Maeterlinck's play *The Blue Bird* at the Theatre Royal, Haymarket, on 8 December 1909 (**77**).

A simple use of colour also became fashionable. 'Jewellery follows the trend of the black and white craze', reported *Vogue* in 1911. 'Black onyx with diamonds or pearls is shown in lovely designs of brooch and locket.'[21] Although black and white had been in vogue at the end of the 19th century, the fashion was encouraged by society mourning for Edward VII, who died in 1910. This stylish combination was created with diamonds on a platinum ground relieved by a chequerboard black pattern of stained chalcedony on a 1913 brooch (**78**), showing the beginnings of the style that would later be known as Art Deco. It was bought from Cartier, New York, in 1913 as a Christmas gift for Julia Appleton Newbold Cross by her husband, the investment banker and early aviator William Redmond Cross. The opening of a branch of Cartier in New York in 1909 allowed American women access to French design without the necessity of a trip to Paris.

Contemporaries such as the French jeweller Robert Carsix characterized this type of jewellery as the alternative to Art Nouveau, noting the use of fine jewels where 'platinum allied with iridium permits the making of extremely fine mounts. The new setting slims the line of the metal even further, giving the impression of a razor's edge.... This is a new formula in the conception of these jewels: everything is sacrificed to highlight the gemstone. It takes the whole space.'[22]

The First World War caused a hiatus in the development of new jewellery: precious metals were required for the war, jewellers were often called up for war work, and there was less demand for jewellery from consumers. However, towards the war's end, *Vogue* noted that 'with the many readjustments of our ideas of life and pleasures and clothes has come a new attitude towards jewellery.... Jewels continue to be worn because they induce cheer and hope...'[23]

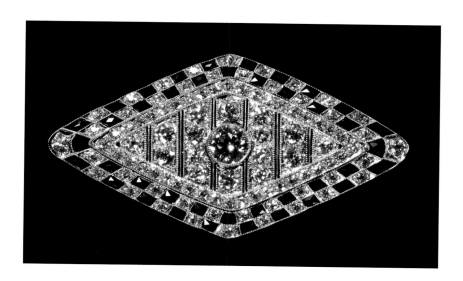

78 Diamonds, stained chalcedony and platinum, by Cartier. Paris, 1913.
M.212-1976. Given by Lady Reigate

CHAPTER FIVE
'Clips are going like wildfire'
1920–1940

The period between the two world wars offered jewellers both opportunities and a feeling of angst. The loss of a generation of young men decimated their customer base, while the effects of industrial unrest, symbolized in Britain by the General Strike of 1926, affected the income of working-class customers as well as those who relied on the profits of shares and industry. The 1929 stock market crash followed by the Great Depression also had a cooling effect on spending. Jewellers were vying for their share of reduced budgets in 'these days of competition when a husband may just as likely give a car to his wife as a piece of jewellery'.[1] At the same time, an air of jittery modernity was sweeping through the world, ushering in an era of smart, modern, streamlined jewels. Platinum, freed from the demands of war production, became the near-invisible foundation for close-set, geometric and densely jewelled brooches. These delicate yet strong platinum settings, which didn't require metal prongs to hold the stones, created, in the words of the New Yorker, jewels which were as 'smooth as a bit of silk and as supple'.[2] The Paris Exposition des Arts Décoratifs et Industriels Modernes of 1925 brought the style later known as Art Deco to public prominence, while the groundbreaking 1929 jewellery exhibition at the Musée Galliera in Paris demonstrated that jewellers had embraced the principles of modern design.

Brooches and clips were the most commonly worn jewels, essential to pin drapery on dresses, fix the folds of soft felt hats, define the V-shape of a décolletage on the front or back of a dress, or hold the loops of a long pearl necklace. In the late 1920s, jewellers invented the clip fitting, folding over a layer of fabric rather than piercing it as a traditional brooch pin would. 'Clips are going like wildfire', claimed the New Yorker in 1933,[3] and the previous year, 'everywhere we hear that clips are still going strong in every form, whether they appear frankly as themselves or are disguised in one way or another. You will see two of them forming a brooch almost anywhere.'[4] Brooches and pins were found in a dizzying array of styles: severe geometric shapes, stylized flowers and baskets of fruit (**80**, **81**), or the modernistic designs of the avant-garde jewellers.

Jewellers worked hard to keep their designs relevant at a time of rapidly changing fashions. Keen to follow the direction of designers and couturiers, they admitted that their jewellery had to chime with new dress fashions. 'The modern girl', they felt in 1927, 'loves jewellery quite as much as her grandmother, but she wants it to fit in with her dress scheme…. The glittering and sparkling surfaces of silk and part-silk materials, the soft tenuousness of the many varieties of crepe, present qualities that have become, in their sudden newness, so satisfying and so complete an effect in themselves that nothing else seems to be wanted. To complete the revolution, the new materials are of such thinness that they will not bear the weight of even a moderate piece of jewellery such as a brooch…. Indeed, the lavish use of gold in brocades, embroideries etc. is a challenge to the very existence of gold in jewellery.'[5] Vogue expanded on the problem of making jewels to suit both plain daywear and the rich fabrics of the evening: 'Sometimes the dress that we wear is so simple that it demands something to stand out, something gay, bold, vif. Or perhaps it is so splendid in the fabric that it requires jewellery that is also brave.'[6]

79 Detail from a photograph of Ava Gardner wearing two diamond clips,
Paramount Theatre, Los Angeles, 1944.
Photo by Bill Dudas/mptvimages.com

80 Enamelled platinum, diamonds, black onyx, carved coral and nephrite jade.
Possibly France, c.1925.
M.126-2007. Given by the American Friends of the V&A through the generosity of Patricia V. Goldstein

81 Platinum, enamelled gold, diamonds, ruby, sapphires, emerald and pearl. UK, 1920–1930.
M.204-2007. Given by the American Friends of the V&A through the generosity of Patricia V. Goldstein

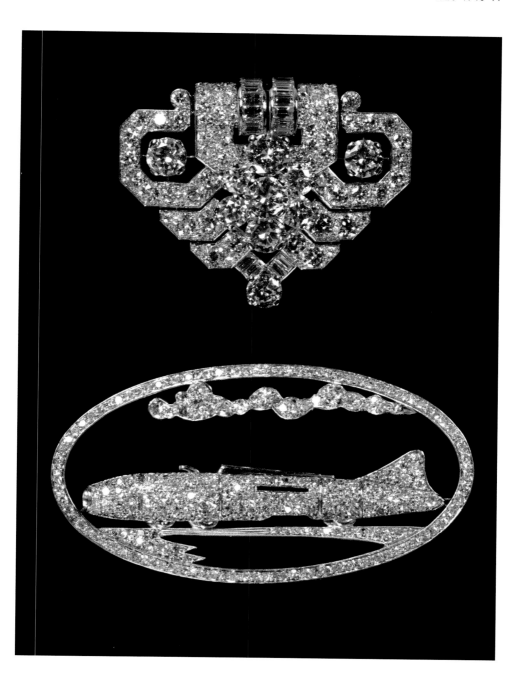

82 Diamond and platinum, by Cartier. London, 1940.
M.36-1994. Bequeathed by Mr and Mrs Ernest Schwaiger

83 Platinum and diamonds. England, 1937.
M.115-1993. Given by Josephine Elwes

84 (left) Platinum, white gold, baguette- and brilliant-cut diamonds, rubies, sapphires
and emerald, by Ostertag. Paris, 1927–40.
M.127-1987. The Bettine, Lady Abingdon Collection. Bequeathed by Mrs T.R.P. Hole

85 (right) White gold, platinum, emeralds, brilliant-cut diamonds and stained chalcedony,
by Lacloche Frères. Paris, c.1927–30.
M.25-1976. Bequeathed by Miss J.H.G. Gollan

Jewellers were presented with the dual challenges of designing brooches and clips that could be worn against the bright, patterned fabrics of 1920s and early '30s women's wear but were also adapted to lighter fabrics and looser, less structured garments. One response to this was to create 'the completely white note' diamond and platinum jewellery described by Georges Fouquet in 1929, the interest supplied by the shape and geometry of the jewel and variety by the mixed cuts of the stones. A diamond and platinum clip given to the actress Adele Dixon, who appeared in the BBC's first television broadcast in 1936, combines diamonds in varied cuts in a geometric framework, which echoes Art Deco architecture (**82**). The oval brooch given by the Rolls-Royce company to the wife of racing driver George Eyston, who broke the World Land Speed record in 1937 in 'Thunderbolt', uses platinum and massed diamonds to create the embodiment of streamlining and speed (**83**).

Diamonds appealed in part because, unlike other gemstones, convincing synthetic substitutes had not been made, but principally because their brilliance and fire 'hold their own against any colour or texture, natural or artificial; in fact the finer the background they are applied to, the better they seem to respond to it'.[7] The monochrome effect could be relieved by touches of colour, added predominantly by sapphires, rubies and emeralds, sometimes carved in the Indian style. A flowering plant in a pot by Ostertag used rounded, cabochon sapphires and rubies and a single carved emerald to relieve the whiteness of the diamonds and platinum (**84**), while a stylized cypress tree pin by Lacloche Frères was given added definition and interest with stained chalcedony and emeralds (**85**). A bow-shaped brooch played on the intersection of fabric and jewels, set with brilliant-cut and the fashionable new baguette-cut diamonds contrasted with stained chalcedony (**86**).

86 Platinum, brilliant- and baguette-cut diamonds, and stained chalcedony.
Europe or USA, 1930–40.
M.120-2007. Given by the American Friends of the V&A
through the generosity of Patricia V. Goldstein

The appeal of the plain palette with a note of colour was felt on both sides of the Atlantic. In December 1929, the *New Yorker* advised that clothing could feature 'the black-on-white-with-one-color idea which gives it simplicity and is not so disturbing to the eye that the personality of the wearer is obscured',[8] while noting that the 'dignity of the long flowing lines of the new silhouette and the return of the feminine vogue has lent new importance to those touches of adornment which every woman loves. Today every costume calls for its own particular touch of color or note of contrast.'[9]

Many jewellers explored the possibilities of less expensive materials to provide that note of colour, such as topaz, lapis lazuli, coral and crystal, since 'practically all semi-precious jewelry is smart at present'.[10] Crystal was reported as 'having a great vogue' in 1934,

although it was noted that 'the trouble with crystal, which inevitably makes it a fad rather than an institution, is that it shatters so easily'.[11] Nevertheless, it appears to great effect in a stylized flower basket brooch made for Cartier, New York, in c.1930 (**87**). An unusual French brooch uses moonstones, opal and mother-of-pearl alongside diamonds and sapphires to create a geometric design, possibly inspired by North African or Native American textiles (**88**).

Versatility was key, as even the richest customers wanted jewels that could be transformed. Double clips became brooches, sometimes joined with a central pin which itself became a stand-alone jewel. Clips were fixed to bracelets, were worn in the centre of a necklace or tiara, or did double service as the jewelled clasp of a bag. Tiny diamond clips could be worn on the lobes of the ears and were, 'the jewellers point out ... equally useful for your lingerie

87 Platinum, rock crystal, baguette- and brilliant-cut diamonds, and moonstone, by Cartier. New York, c.1930.
M.130-2007. Given by the American Friends of the V&A through the generosity of Patricia V. Goldstein

straps (*there's* something)'.[12] Adaptable fixings made this possible, although the Paris firm of Mauboussin (perhaps with an eye to sales) felt that no jewel should be wearable more than two ways.[13]

'Women of original taste', according to the *Goldsmiths' Journal* in 1927, were 'wearing jewellery in a new way. Brooches are commonly used on the shoulder or as hat ornaments. Hints may be had for nothing at any social function.'[14] Hats provided an adaptable surface for brooches, either as hat pins or, as the Duchess of Westminster explained, 'In the autumn of 1925 we wore pairs of little diamanté animals in our felt hats. Otherwise we pinned real brooches to them, which was asking for trouble as they were always falling off or getting stolen in cloakrooms.'[15] Credit for this fashion was given to the five-times-married Lady Idina Hay, known as 'the Bolter'.[16]

A striking diamond and platinum hat pin with contrasting coral and stained chalcedony fan shapes resembles the Cartier 'cliquet' pin, in which the end of the pin detached, allowing the point to pass through the hat, leaving only the decorative elements visible (**89**).

In 1930, the *New Yorker* reported that 'the trinket which is taking all the ladies' hearts this year is the clip-watch. It looks exactly like the usual ornamental clip-on you've seen clamped to so many necklines, or cuffs or gowns; but concealed among the jewels is a tiny watch, which snaps up on a hinge when one wants to know the time.'[17] The clip or brooch watch allowed watches to be worn with evening dress without spoiling the overall effect of the costume. This idea was elegantly executed in Paris by Lacloche Frères in a black and red brooch watch, the colour and design inspired by Asian art (**90**).

88 Platinum, gold, diamonds, mother-of-pearl, common light opal, moonstones and sapphires. France, 1920–30.
M.132-2007. Given by the American Friends of the V&A through the generosity of Patricia V. Goldstein

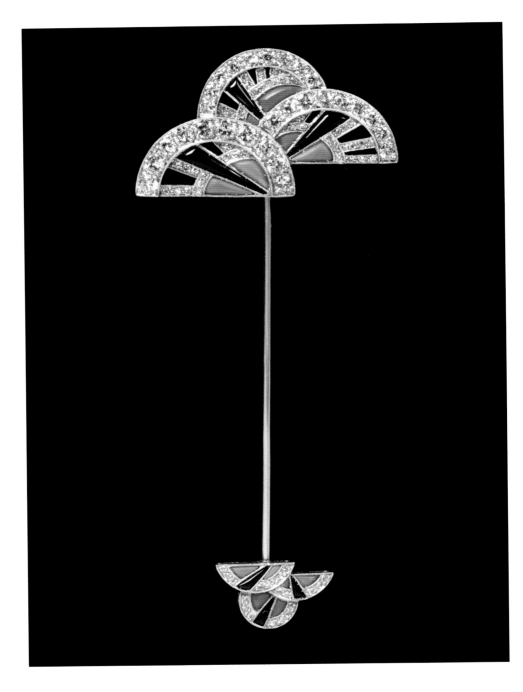

89 Platinum, coral, stained chalcedony and brilliant-cut diamonds.
Europe or USA, c.1920–30.
M.128-2007. Given by the American Friends of the V&A
through the generosity of Patricia V. Goldstein

90 Gold, platinum, enamel, brilliant- and rose-cut diamonds, sapphires, jadeite, black-backed chalcedony, pearl and silk (front and back shown), by Lacloche Frères. Paris, c.1930.
M.170-2007. Given by the American Friends of the V&A
through the generosity of Patricia V. Goldstein

91 White gold, brilliant-cut diamonds, black enamel and coral,
by Raymond Templier. Paris, c.1930.
M.134-2007. Given by the American Friends of the V&A
through the generosity of Patricia V. Goldstein

92 White gold, lapis lazuli and blue glass,
by Raymond Templier. France, 1934.
M.18-1979. © ADAGP, Paris and DACS, London 2019

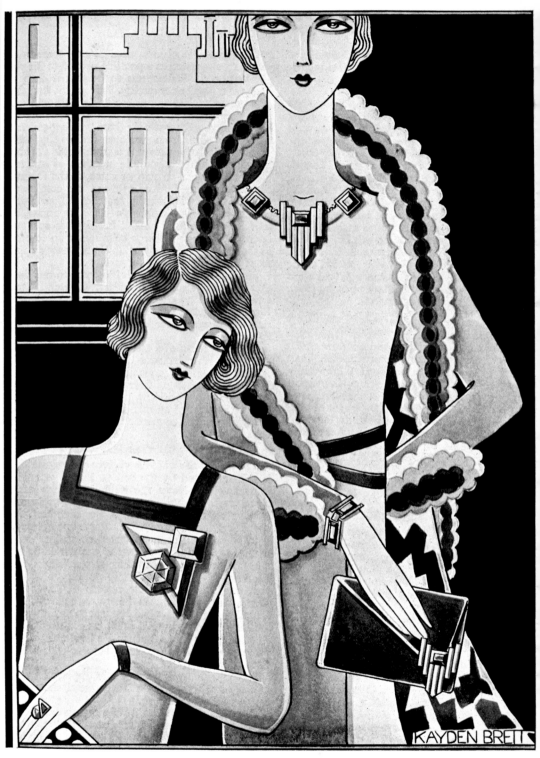

Jewellery for the Business Woman

By the 1930s jewellers were encouraged by the move to longer, more draping dresses. As the *Goldsmiths' Journal* explained to its readers: 'It will be difficult for a woman to live up to the romance of the old styles without a judiciously selected piece of jewellery. Flowing dresses need as the finishing touch the ring, brooch or chain which if proper care is given to their selection stamp the wearer as essentially a "feminine woman".'[18]

A group of jewellers working outside the mainstream jewellery houses created jewels inspired by the modern world around them, taking inspiration from the city, cars, airplanes, machinery. Artists including Gérard Sandoz, Raymond Templier and Jean Fouquet formed the Union des Artistes Modernes in 1929. Their manifesto set out their goals concisely: 'Jewellery today, directly inspired by our contemporary aesthetic, must be simple, plain, constructed without frills.'[19] Two brooches by Templier illustrate his mastery of these principles: one is a composition of black enamel, coral and diamonds (**91**), while the other cleverly balances two curved blue volumes of glass and lapis lazuli (**92**), or, as contemporary Gaston Varenne noted, 'shadow and light, carefully calculated'.[20] Not everyone appreciated the new style. The critic Robert de la Sizeranne bemoaned the way that 'our rings look like taximeters and our brooches like the square on the hypotenuse'.[21] The fashion for modern, geometric jewellery made it into mainstream design: an illustration from the *Goldsmiths' Journal* in March 1930 shows a very large jade and jet brooch set with a faceted stone (**93**). As the journal asked: 'Why should not the Business Woman try a change of jewellery?'[22]

By 1935 the fashion in brooches had swung towards even greater flamboyance in design and, in particular, the use of gold: 'Since the price of gold has risen, there has been a complete upset in the jewellery market; gold is in fashion again, and is being used with the most expensive stones. Because they are at their best against a background of gold, rubies are in style, and because rubies have become popular, there is also a yen for other colored stones, such as topaz, aquamarine and tourmaline. It's a sort of vicious circle and we rather like it.'[23] Observers noted a return to more floral, ornamented styles or, as the *Sheffield Daily Independent* put it in 1938, 'a movement away from the simple and severe in the direction of the decorative, the romantic and the ornamental'.[24] Jewellery was increasing in size; large single stones or clusters of stones in invisible settings created a solid mass of colour. Double clip brooches continued to be popular and added a note of brightness to plainer fabrics and tailored suits (**79**). On 'dresses which tend to rely for their effect on the gleam and sparkle of a clasp at the neck', *The Gemmologist* reported in March 1938, 'the double device is one to be widely welcomed'.[25]

93 Drawing showing a geometric jet, stone and jade brooch 'especially suitable' for the business woman. *Goldsmiths' Journal*, March 1930

CHAPTER SIX

'Almost anything goes'
1940–1960

The beginnings of the Second World War disrupted the jewellery trade in Europe and, to a less pronounced effect, the United States.[1] Government controls on gold began in Germany in 1939, and Jewish jewellers and gemstone cutters were placed under severe restrictions.[2] By 1940 British factories making costume jewellery, as well as the firms making fine jewellery, had turned to war production. The manufacture of new jewellery in Britain was banned under the Utility regulations, with the sole exception of 9-carat-gold wedding rings and jewellery intended for export. American jewellers, if not called up to fight, were occupied making service medals. Platinum was exclusively for use in industry and munitions, copper was restricted, and gold was required to pay for essential imports. Despite this, jewellery continued to play its small part in keeping up civilian morale. As the New Yorker remarked in 1943, a woman still welcomed 'a giddy lapel ornament with earrings to match … these foolish things are often all that is needed to make an old dress or suit seem new again, not only to the beholder but to the wearer'.[3]

Men were a disappointment to the jeweller when it came to brooches and pins. In 1939 it was reported that men 'to their great detriment had to a great extent given up on wearing jewellery, and the desire of modern man seemed to be to make himself inconspicuous'.[4] After all, 'what was wanted was to make it fashionable to wear more jewellery. How many men', the reporter asked, 'now wore a scarf pin?'

A patriotic note crept into brooches either through the use of red, white and blue stones or more overtly in the shape of flags. A brooch shaped like a Stars and Stripes flying in the breeze was a discreet note of support for the troops (**95**), though contemporaries in 1940 were undecided about such an obvious gesture: 'You'll have to decide for yourself how you feel about American flags on lapels, we're not taking sides.'[5] A small brooch with a single blue star in the centre represented a Service Flag, flown by American families who had members serving in the military (**96**). Each star stood for a serving family member and would be replaced by a gold star if the soldier died. In France, Jeanne Toussaint designed brooches for Cartier in the form of caged birds to protest the Nazi occupation of Paris, while dress designer Elsa Schiaparelli wore a phoenix brooch as her own 'Symbol of France'.[6]

The American firm of Trabert & Hoeffer-Mauboussin found an ingenious way to make interesting jewellery available at lower prices. Their line of 'Reflection' jewellery, first created in 1938, was made by assembling prefabricated cast parts in an arrangement chosen by the customer. One 'Reflection' brooch is set with fashionable soft moonstones and sapphire beads, and shows the rounded curves and asymmetry in vogue in the 1940s and '50s; white gold offered an alternative to platinum, which remained in short supply (**97**).

The years immediately after the war presented further difficulties. Rebuilding the shattered cities and societies of continental Europe required continued rationing and, in the UK, the luxury tax on jewellery rose as high as 125%, making new jewellery almost unaffordable. Nevertheless, the jewellery trade did its best to

94 Cover of LIFE magazine, 28 April 1941, showing a bakelite heart and key brooch, perhaps a reference to wartime separations.
Photo: George Karger, The LIFE Images Collection via Getty Images

LIFE

S RIGHT

APRIL 28, 1941 **10** CENTS
YEARLY SUBSCRIPTION **$4.50**

OFF.

95 Platinum, diamonds, rubies and sapphires. USA, c.1940–45.
M.218-2007. Given by the American Friends of the V&A
through the generosity of Patricia V. Goldstein

96 Platinum, diamonds, rubies and sapphire. USA, c.1940–45.
M.219-2007. Given by the American Friends of the V&A
through the generosity of Patricia V. Goldstein

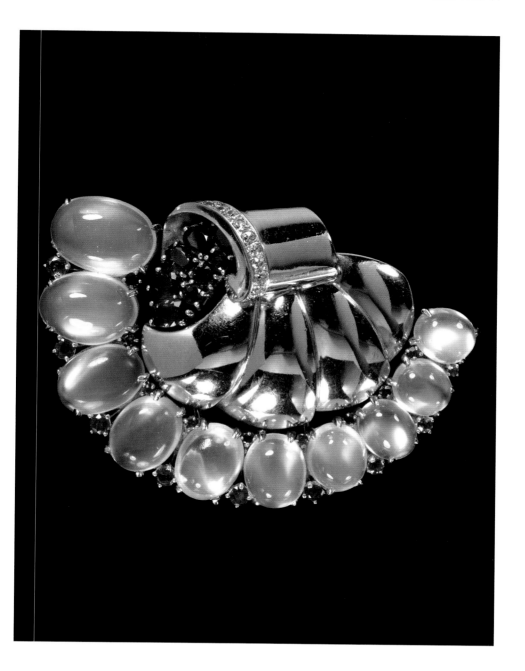

97 White gold, sapphires, diamonds and moonstones,
by Trabert & Hoeffer-Mauboussin. USA, c.1940.
M.168-1978

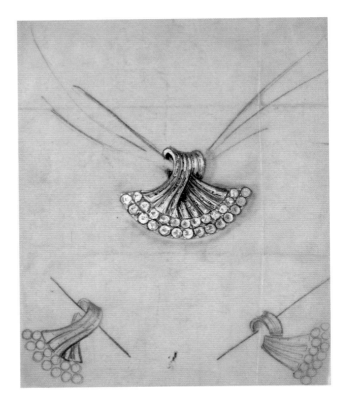

continue. Fashion moved towards softer, rounded designs with a greater use of fantasy and whimsy. The properties of gold were exploited to create interesting textural effects, and brooches continued to be used to reflect current events, add a splash of colour and brilliance to costume, or create an amusing conversational point. In 1949 the *New Yorker* assured its readers that, 'as far as design is concerned, almost anything goes this year; you can be as conventional or as whimsical as you please.... We might remark that there is also a definite inclination towards irregularity of design.'[7] Brooches often still separated into pairs of clips (**98**), 'like an amoeba only much more expensively',[8] but these were now likely to be asymmetrical. Gorgeously coloured birds, butterflies, fish and even flies were made into brooches; according to Paris magazine *Femina*, the year 1945 should be placed under the sign of wings (**99**).[9]

The 1950s, for many countries, was a period of optimism. Fashions in dress became more flowing and generous; jewellery followed with rounder curves, scrolls and the use of large gemstones rather than pavé settings that required expensive workmanship. Floral motifs became increasingly fashionable, following the spirit of femininity shown in dress. A brooch designed by Jean Schlumberger for Tiffany used polished sapphires and gold to create a bouquet of flowers tied with a diamond bow-knot (**100**), and another used sapphire and emerald beads to make a pair of pine cones (**101**).

98 Design for a diamond double clip, separating into two smaller clips.
Godman and Rabey Archive, London, c. 1940–50.
AAD/209/1/v5. Given by Alan Rabey

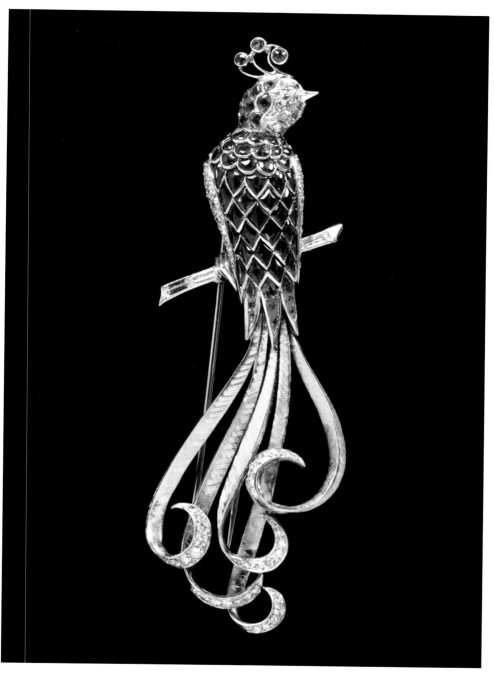

99 Gold, platinum, yellow and colourless diamonds, emeralds,
rubies and sapphires. France, 1940–50.
M.121-2007. Given by the American Friends of the V&A
through the generosity of Patricia V. Goldstein

100 Gold, sapphires and diamonds, designed by Jean Schlumberger
for Tiffany & Co. New York, c.1950–60.
M.153-2007. Given by the American Friends of the V&A
through the generosity of Patricia V. Goldstein

101 Gold, platinum, diamonds, emeralds and sapphires, designed
by Jean Schlumberger for Tiffany & Co. New York, 1950–60.
M.137-2007. Given by the American Friends of the V&A
through the generosity of Patricia V. Goldstein

'A second trend is the increasing popularity of gold studded with diamonds. The stones range in size from chips to solitaires', reported the *New Yorker* in 1952.[10] Gold was used in its own right rather than principally as a support for gemstones: 'If the gold is jewelled ... you'll find that the jewels are generally used to complement the gold this season rather than the other way round (if it is the jewel you want to complement, the idea is to use a platinum setting, because platinum is strong enough to permit a setting so unobtrusive as to be practically invisible).'[11]

Jewellers explored new ways of working with gold, creating engraved finishes that looked like cloth, gold mesh, latticework or a twisted-wire rope pattern. A pair of dress clips from Van Cleef & Arpels show gold pleated into soft folds and topped with nail-head-like diamonds (**102**), while Chaumet used twisted gold wire and diamonds to create overlapping plumes (**103**). A brooch from Van Cleef & Arpels was made as a fashionable, asymmetric bow-knot (**104**).

Brooches and lapel pins often reflected events in the wider world. A gold and diamond brooch (**105**) commemorates the first diesel locomotive to be used by the American Lehigh Valley Railroad, running from New Jersey to Buffalo. The line was set up to transport anthracite coal (known as 'black diamonds'), and the flagship train shown on this brooch was known as the 'Diamond'. This brooch may have been made as a gift for the wife of one of the railway engineers or investors, although jewels inspired by cars, planes and trains were widely fashionable. The American firm Verdura showed a 'gold locomotive with a diamond headlight, jewelled coal in the tender and two day coaches' lapel pin in 1941.[12]

The 'Sputnik' brooch, with its fierce, spiky design, is a reminder of the feverish Space Race of the mid-twentieth century; the excitement and, for Americans, dismay caused by the launch of the Russian 'Sputnik' orbiter in 1957.[13] Jewellery inspired by space, comets and molecular models burst onto the scene (**106**).

102 Gold and diamonds, by Van Cleef & Arpels. Paris, 1955.
M.34&A-1983

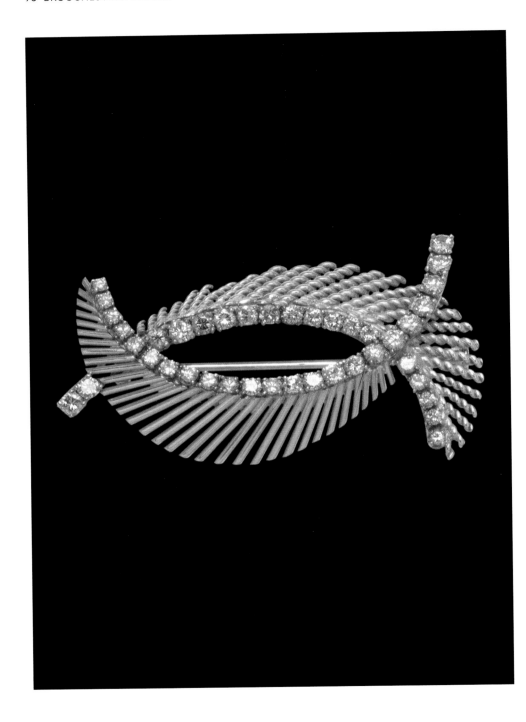

103 Gold and diamonds, by Chaumet. London, 1950–55.
M.120-1987. The Bettine, Lady Abingdon Collection, bequeathed by Mrs T.R.P. Hole

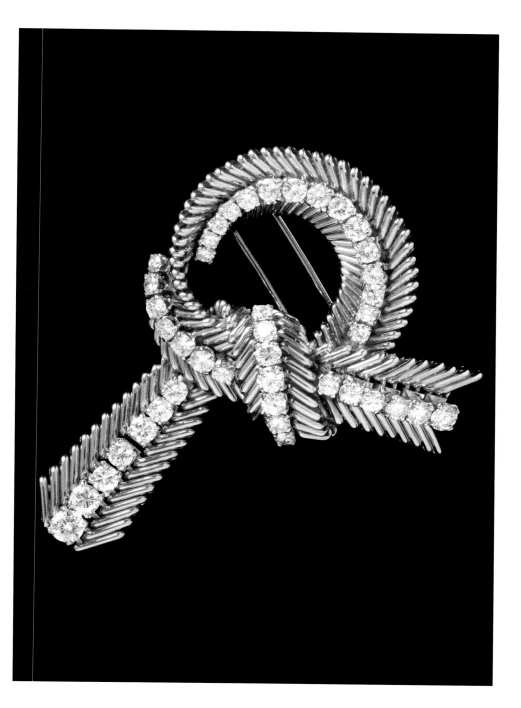

104 Gold and diamonds, by Van Cleef & Arpels. Paris, 1960.
M.135-2007. Given by the American Friends of the V&A
through the generosity of Patricia V. Goldstein

105 Gold, diamonds, sapphires and rock crystal. USA, c.1948.
M.169-2007. Given by the American Friends of the V&A
through the generosity of Patricia V. Goldstein

106 Gold, by Cartier. New York, c.1958.
LOAN: MET ANON.5-2007. Lent through the generosity of
William & Judith, and Douglas and James Bollinger

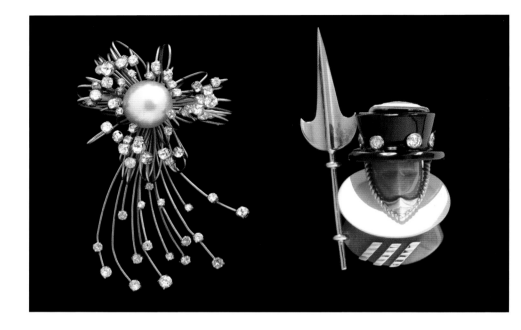

Costume jewellery became even more popular in the 1950s, offering bright colours at affordable prices and, as *Vogue* reported of the Givenchy couture collection in 1959, the 'secret of lightness': 'All the pins feel like feathers in the hand (or the hair or dress) ... made of ersatz crystals in a new floating feather weight.'[14] A comet-shaped brooch (**107**) brought space-inspired jewellery to those with modest budgets.

In 1956, the *New Yorker* reported that 'if there is any new trend to be detected in the smithies this fall, it is that everything seems to be a trifle more empathic than it was a year ago. The splendor is a bit more splendid, the sentimentality a bit more sentimental, and the nonsense a bit more nonsensical.'[15] Lapel pins in the shape of animals, objects or cartoon figures added a note of humour to costumes. Cartier

specialized in such figures – 'chalcedony, a milk white stone that is a cousin of agate, is the nucleus of a number of small lapel pins'[16] – such as a brooch in which semi-precious stones form the head and bust of a uniformed British Yeoman of the Guard (**108**). Cartier made these Beefeater brooches for a number of years, but they took on a particular appeal around the coronation of Elizabeth II in 1953.

An interesting brooch could not only entertain the wearer but could also serve a useful social function, as explained by a 1961 advertisement for jewellers F.J. Cooper showing a pin in the shape of a fly: 'A customer we know wears hers on the back of her dress at parties. She reports it's an uncanny way to start – and sometimes stop – conversation.'[17] Hollywood jeweller Paul Flato made a number of jewels based on shoes and feet, including jewelled pom-pom sandals,

107 (left) Metal, glass, pastes and imitation pearl. France, c.1950.
T.130-1970

108 (right) Gold, coral, chalcedony, onyx and diamonds, by Cartier. Paris, c.1955.
M.177:1-2007. Given by the American Friends of the V&A
through the generosity of Patricia V. Goldstein

slippers and cowboy boots. According to his obituary in the *New York Times*, the pair of little gold feet with ruby toenails were originally made for the dancer Irene Castle as a nod to her career and a play on her maiden name of Foote (**109**); they offered a surreal touch when pinned to the lapel. In comparison, the unicorn's head brooch designed for the couturier Christian Dior presents a light-hearted detail (**110**). Dior's affordable jewellery was designed to be updated as fashions changed. He declared in 1956, 'As always with fashion, good taste is more important than money. Some women just keep on wearing brooches in the same old place, on their collars or the lapels of their suits. Other women, however, blessed with a sense of fashion, take the same brooch and use it to attach a colored scarf to the hip pocket of their suits – this looks marvellous and is twice as effective. Costume jewellery is

entirely different from real jewellery and must be worn for what it is.'[18]

Jewellery made by artists presented an alternative to the creations of the major jewellery houses. Seen as 'wearable art', it allowed the designer to express his or her artistic vision in both traditional and non-traditional materials. A gold brooch in the shape of a fish was made by the German goldsmith Elisabeth Treskow (**111**). She was strongly influenced by ancient jewellery, of which she had an important collection, and used the Etruscan technique of granulation to decorate the surface of the brooch. Though the design uses gold, pearl and sapphire, the finished effect is individual and modern.

Artists and jewellers working in the craft tradition replaced the polished finish and exquisite technique of professional jewellers with a

109 (left) Gold and rubies, by Paul Flato. USA, 1940–50.
M.173:1, 2-2007. Given by the American Friends of the V&A through the generosity of Patricia V. Goldstein

110 (right) Gilt metal and cut glass, designed by Mitchel Maer for Christian Dior.
England, c.1950.
M.25-1988. Given by Stephen Maer

spirit of experimentation. As the American jeweller Sam Kramer explained in the 1950s: 'Experimentation ... with metals, materials, gems, tools, and techniques is doubtlessly the life flow of jewelry as a creative expression.'[19] The sculptor Alexander Calder made jewellery from early childhood, largely to give to family and friends. His work was often in brass or steel wire, using strong, simple shapes. When displayed at the Willard Gallery in New York in 1940, it was described as 'half savage and half surrealist'.[20] The success of one brooch made in the 1950s (**112**) depends on its pleasing shape

more than any intrinsic value.[21] A gold brooch by the Italian sculptor Arnaldo Pomodoro shows an arrangement of twisted, almost haphazard gold and silver forms (**113**).

In 1962, De Beers urged its customers that each 'pin, clip or brooch should be chosen to be very personally yours, a bit of glory you can wear with almost everything you own'.[22] Whether a finely made gem-set piece, a cheaper costume jewellery pin or the work of an avant-garde artist, each jewel reflected the life and aesthetic choices of its owner.

111 Gold, diamonds, sapphire and baroque pearl, by Elisabeth Treskow. Cologne, 1953.
M.1-1988

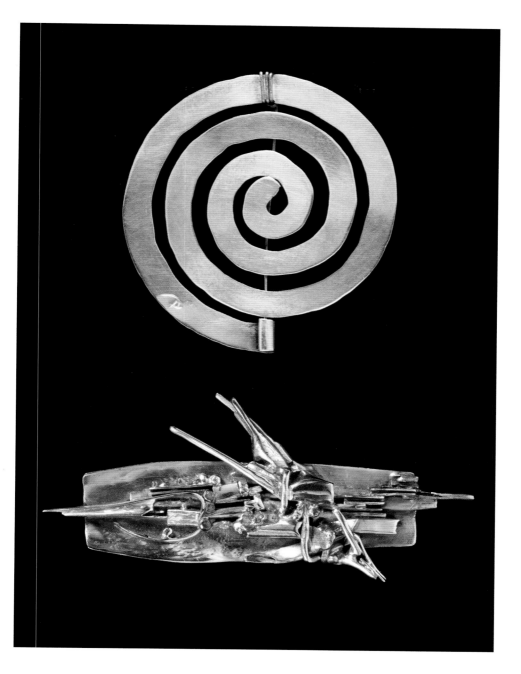

112 Brass, by Alexander Calder. USA, 1950–60.
M.166-2007. Given by the American Friends of the V&A through the generosity of Patricia V. Goldstein.
© 2019 Calder Foundation, New York/DACS, London

113 Gold and silver, by Arnaldo Pomodoro. Italy, 1958.
CIRC.63-1960

CHAPTER SEVEN

'Precious stones have won their freedom'
1960–1990

'Time was when precious stones were nearly always cut to fit formal, balanced, rigid settings and only such freakishly shaped jewels as fresh-water pearls forced the designer to create settings around them. Of late, though, precious stones have won their freedom – a freedom that in some cases seems to verge on license or even downright delinquency', claimed the *New Yorker* in 1957.[1] The range of materials used in jewellery had widened enormously and, while many jewellers in the 1960s and '70s continued to work with gemstones, it was often in their crystal form or in rough, irregular cuts. The increase in jewellers trained at the major art schools brought in new ideas from the art world and a spirit of experimentation.

A large brooch of almost barbaric splendour by New York jeweller Arthur King is set with slices of watermelon tourmaline in a fluid, abstract gold mount (**115**). A brooch by his British counterpart, Andrew Grima, is an exuberant sunburst of gold, set with a dome of polished lapis lazuli surrounded by turquoise drops (**116**). Both men came to jewellery through unconventional routes. King was a self-taught jeweller who learnt to work with metal by practising on scraps while serving in the US Navy during the Second World War. Grima was working in his father-in-law's jewellery business when a chance encounter with two dealers carrying a suitcase of exotically coloured Brazilian gemstones set him on his creative path. In 1961, Grima was asked to make pieces designed by artists such as Elisabeth Frink and Kenneth Armitage for the International Exhibition of Modern Jewellery in London's Goldsmiths' Hall.

He presented his own collection to the art director Graham Hughes and subsequently won a series of design awards. Both Grima and King boasted dazzling flagship stores and illustrious clients. Grima's lapis and turquoise brooch was bought by the film director Roman Polanski as a wedding anniversary gift for his wife, Sharon Tate.

Jewellers at this time were inspired not only by the shapes and colours of gemstones but also by the wider natural world. Grima cast jewels directly from volcanic lava, as well as leaves and lichen which he collected near his home. One astonishingly naturalistic jewel by John Donald was actually cast from a piece of honeycomb and set with a fire opal and diamond bee (**117**). Due to the fragile nature of the honeycomb, it took two years of constant experimentation to perfect the design.[2] The idea came from a collaboration with the sculptor and author Michael Ayrton.[3] In Ayrton's 1967 novel *The Maze Maker*, the Greek inventor Daedalus is challenged to make a gold honeycomb with seven bees. He realizes that the honeycomb is 'the only creation in nature which is itself a wax model and one more delicately constructed than any man could achieve',[4] and he uses the comb as the base for a lost-wax casting. When a New Zealand patron commissioned Ayrton to make a gold model using this method, he enlisted the help of John Donald, who subsequently adopted the process to make a series of honeycomb jewels.

A brooch shaped like a pair of sycamore seeds – the result of a collaboration between the

114 Andrew Logan, dressed half as sailor, half as mermaid, wearing a fish brooch with suspended swags of chain, 1985. Studio shot for the 6th Alternative Miss World. Make-up by Phyllis Cohen. Female costume by Zandra Rhodes.
Photo: Robyn Beeche

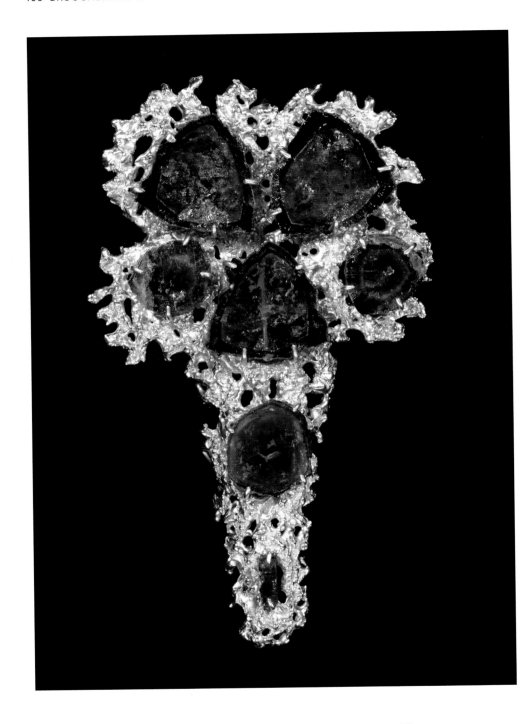

115 Gold and watermelon tourmalines, by Arthur King. USA, c.1970.
M.21-2006. Given by Joan Hurst through the Art Fund

116 Gold, platinum, lapis lazuli, turquoise and diamonds,
by Andrew Grima. London, 1967–8.
M.34-2009. Given by William and Judith Bollinger

117 Gold, diamonds, citrine and Mexican fire opals, by John Donald.
London, 1969.
M.14-2006. Given by Joan Hurst through the Art Fund

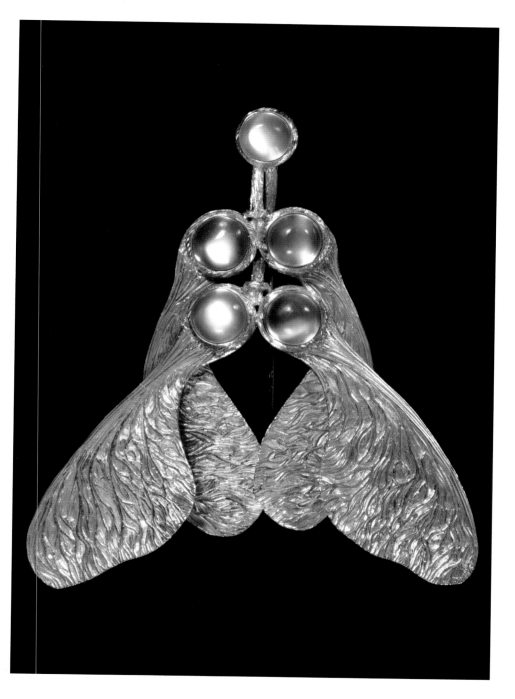

118 Gold and moonstones, designed and engraved by Malcolm Appleby
and made by Roger Doyle. London, 1975.
M.314-1977

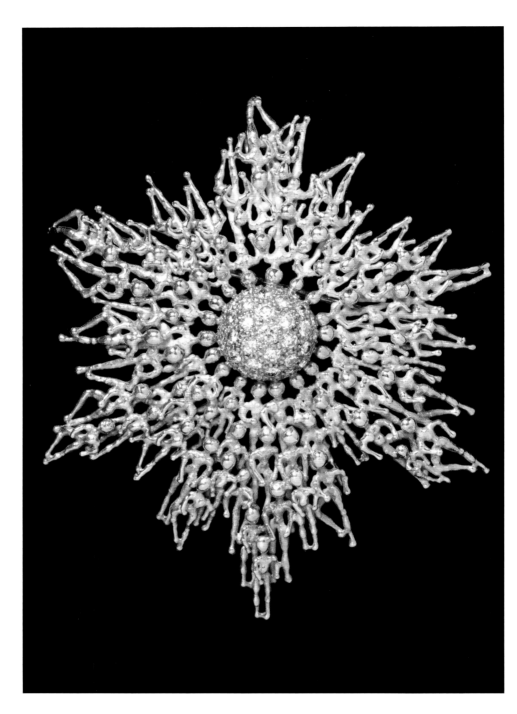

119 Gold and diamonds, by Stuart Devlin. England, c.1972.
M.18-2006. Given by Joan Hurst through the Art Fund

engraver Malcolm Appleby and jeweller Roger Doyle – was also closely based on nature; the carefully textured engraving on the surface of the 'wings' gives a feeling of glamorous naturalism (**118**). After finishing his studies at the Royal College of Art in London, Appleby bought a disused railway station in Scotland and set up a studio, working on commissions as varied as the coronet for the Prince of Wales's investiture and an orb marking the first moonwalk.

At first glance, Stuart Devlin's gold and diamond brooch (**119**) appears to be a loosely formed starburst, but closer examination reveals a disconcerting array of tiny naked figures raying out from a diamond-studded centre. In 1958, the Australian-born Devlin received a scholarship to attend the Royal College of Art, which he described as 'the pinnacle of the system'.[5] Although many of the schools were still housed in condemned Nissan huts left over from the war years, the RCA buzzed with creative energy and excitement, and Devlin's contemporaries included the renowned painter David Hockney and fashion designer Mary Quant. He became involved with

the sculpture, ceramics and industrial design schools – all influences which followed him in his work.

Elizabeth Gage studied at the Sir John Cass College, also in London, and a rival centre for jewellery and goldsmithing. Rather than the experimental goldwork that many of her contemporaries used, Gage was inspired by the forms and polished cabochon stones of medieval and Renaissance jewellery. She called her 1972–3 brooch (**120**) one of her 'classic kiss-style pins' because of the diagonal cross formed by the four small pearls in the centre. She described her jewellery as creating a memory, the wearer reliving how they bought it and where they wore it.

The increasing number of art schools teaching jewellery in the 1960s created a new wave of practitioners and challenged the idea that jewellers were principally 'makers of luxury objects from precious metals that functioned as adornment for the body'.[6] In 1961, the V&A collaborated with Graham Hughes to organize 'the world's first international exhibition of

120 Gold, enamel, tourmalines, aquamarines, rubies and cultured pearls, by Elizabeth Gage. London, 1972–3.
M.20:1-2010. Given by Elizabeth Gage

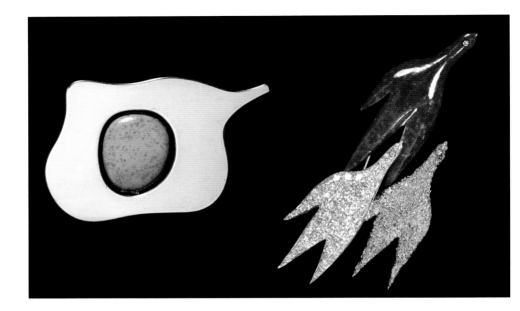

modern artists' jewellery'.[7] It aimed to give new life to the British jewellery industry, which was still recovering from the austerity of the post-war years and the effects of high purchase taxes. Jewellers were invited to submit work, as were contemporary sculptors and artists, whose wax models were cast by H.J. Company and the sculpture school at the Royal College of Art. The intention was to showcase creativity in jewellery and bring it closer to the spirit of innovation and iconoclasm that was sweeping the art world at the time. The Surrealist artist Jean Arp, for example, displayed a silver brooch set with a speckled pebble, which was made from his designs by the Israeli jeweller Johanan Peter (**121**). The amorphous shape was derived from Arp's interest in biomorphism: using abstract forms to evoke plants or living cells.

A bird brooch representing the three sons of Eos, the Ancient Greek goddess of the dawn, was also the result of an artistic collaboration

(**122**). Jeweller Heger de Löwenfeld made the brooch based on a Braque lithograph, roughening the surface of the gold to emulate the sand that Braque mixed into his paints.

The rise of casual, youth-orientated fashion caused the role of brooches as essential adjuncts to dress to be weakened, but, at the same time, the pictorial surface offered by brooches and their prominent placement on clothing allowed for their role as artworks and means of self-expression to grow. As an early member of a crafts society, the collector and gallery owner Helen Drutt, explained: 'When I went to the meetings, if I wanted to talk about the crafts, I couldn't carry in a Nakashima table or a big ceramic pot, but I could wear a brooch that evoked the same information, or acted as a catalyst.... The jewelry was no different from the furniture or other crafts. It was just a vehicle that was more affordable and more portable.'[8]

121 (left) Silver and pebble, designed by Jean Arp and made by Johanan Peter. Israel, 1960.
CIRC.395-1962. Given by the maker. © DACS 2019

122 (right) Lapis lazuli, gold, platinum and pavé-set diamonds, designed by Georges Braque
and made by Heger de Löwenfeld. France, 1963.
M.5-1992. © ADAGP, Paris and DACS, London 2019

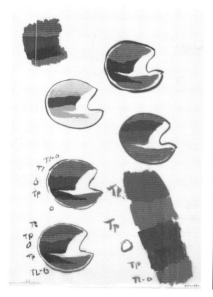

Some of this generation of jewellers turned away from traditional metals and gemstones in favour of modern materials such as aluminium, rubber, textiles, plastics and acrylic. Susanna Heron's 'flying bird' brooch, for example, uses scarlet resin inlaid in silver in an abstract form that suggests a bird flying across a red sky (**123**, **124**). Heron was interested in making jewellery which was affordable and accessible to a wide group of people, and thereby injected art into everyday life. Trained on a jewellery course at the Central School of Art and Design in London, she found that she had to look outside the school to find the facilities to work with less traditional materials such as resin.[9]

American artist and jewellery maker Elsa (also known as Elsie) Freund pioneered a method to fuse broken window glass or coloured bottles to clay, which she then set in hammered silver mounts to create bold, colourful jewels that her husband christened 'Elsaramics' (**125**). Her training as a painter gave her a sophisticated sense of colour but, as a self-taught jeweller, Freund developed her methods through trial and error.[10] The low cost of the materials she used certainly made her jewellery accessible and, as she did not know how to price it, her earlier pieces were costed according to local plumber day rates.[11]

Similarly, Thomas Gentille's brooch (**126**) takes the humblest of materials and creates a sophisticated, minimalist jewel. For this piece he used a traditional Japanese technique to set shards of broken eggshell in wet lacquer. Gentille's embrace of commonplace materials has also included 'ivory from piano keys, sawdust, resin, pumice, dyed cork, wood and a specific industrial silver paint usually used on mirrors'.[12]

Arline Fisch's 'Black Floating Square' (**127**) is a jewel as versatile as the clip brooches of the

123 (left) Working drawing for 'flying bird' brooch (**124**), in gouache on tracing paper, by Susanna Heron. UK, 1975.
CIRC.389-1976. © Susanna Heron. All rights reserved, DACS 2019
124 (right) Silver and resin, by Susanna Heron. London, 1975.
M.181-1976

125 Silver and glass fused to ceramic, by Elsa Freund. USA, 1967.
M.11:1-1992. Given by Mrs H. Libby West

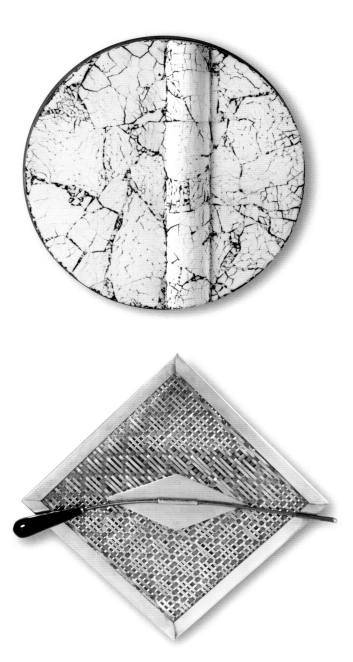

126 Ostrich eggshell, wood, bronze and gold, by Thomas Gentille. New York, c.1982.
M.2-1988. Given by the artist

127 Woven gold and silver, and black onyx, by Arline Fisch. USA, 1987.
M.19 to C-1989

1920s and '30s, able to be worn both as a brooch and as part of a bracelet. Fisch pioneered the use of textile techniques in metalwork, knitting, weaving and knotting gold, silver and copper-plated wire into jewels that bridged the gap between jewellery and clothing. She taught both weaving and jewellery at San Diego State College in the 1960s, and was first inspired to use textile techniques in jewellery making when she saw pre-Columbian metalwork in Peru. Her aim was for her jewellery to act as an icebreaker. As she explained, 'If someone's wearing a piece of art jewelry, something that is out of the ordinary, the tendency is for people to comment on it ... and that provokes an interaction.'[13]

'Athene Noctua' (**128**) displays Kevin Coates's technical mastery as well as his interest in myth and literature and the influence of his studies in mathematics and geometry. Here, the head of the Greek goddess Athena is set against a blued titanium sky. Her sacred bird, the Little Owl or *Athene Noctua*, perches on her helmet. American artist William Harper shares Coates's interest in imagery and symbolism (**129**) but creates jewels in a very different style. He uses the technique of cloisonné enamel, in which a design is created with thin strips of wire into which colourful enamels are inlaid, to make jewels inspired by Asian and Central American art, African assemblage art and found objects. The title of the brooch, 'The Virgin and the Unicorn', refers to medieval legends in which the fierce unicorn can only be tamed by a virgin. Harper also expected courage from the wearers of his jewels: 'I'm trying to build into the work a kind of amuletic, talismanic quality

128 (left) Blued titanium, gold, silver and platinum, by Kevin Coates.
London, 1983.
M.19-1983. Commissioned by the V&A

129 (right) Gold, silver, lead, cloisonné enamel, tourmalines, pearls
and amethyst, by William Harper. USA, 1988.
M.3-1990

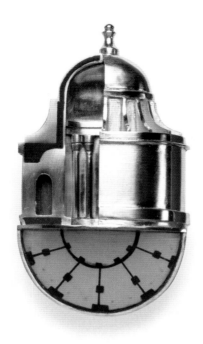

130 Silver, gold and Perspex, by Vicki Ambery-Smith.
London, 1980.
M.40-1982

131 Yellow gold and silver, partly oxidized and painted, by Fritz Maierhofer.
London, 1987.
M.65-1988

132 Mirrored glass, glitter and resin, by Andrew Logan. England, 1985.
M.55-2003. Given by Janine du Plessis

133 Lithographs on paper, plastic and metal. UK, 1970s.
E.626-2002. Purchased through the Julie and Robert Breckman Print Fund

that requires an element of bravery on the part of the owner in order to wear it – the work is strong and the wearer is strong.'[14]

Both Vicki Ambery-Smith and Fritz Maierhofer took inspiration from architecture (**130**, **131**). Ambery-Smith's brooch looks back at Renaissance building: the design appears to be loosely based on an architectural drawing by Bramante showing the floorplan and internal structure of the Tempietto in St Peter's Church in Montorio, Rome. Maierhofer's reading of architecture creates a very different impression. His forms are based on the steel girders and materials he saw when working in London at the height of the 1980s construction boom. The modular, mass-produced elements of industrial construction are used in the service of a hand-made brooch, which emphasizes the space and internal structure of a building rather than its mass and external appearance.

The art collector Blanche Brown explained why she bought a brooch by the studio jeweller Ed Weiner in the 1940s: 'It looked great. I could afford it and it identified me with the group of my choice, aesthetically aware, intellectually inclined and politically progressive. That pin (or one of a few others like it) was our badge and we wore it proudly.'[15] This impulse governed both the wearers of Andrew Logan's pins (**114**) and those who bought the multitude of lapel badges made in the second half of the century. Each used their choice of brooch or badge to affiliate themselves with their chosen group and to make a public display of their sympathies. A brooch in the shape of a fish covered with glitter and mirrored glass subverted both the tradition of fine jewellery and the idea of beauty contests (**132**). It was made by Logan and given by him to one of the organizers of the 1985 'Alternative Miss World' event, attended by gay activists and artists, for which the theme was Water.[16]

Just as the limited supply of hand-made artist brooches served to make Blanche Brown feel part of an exclusive, intimate group, so the large-scale production of cheap, easily manufactured lapel badges made their wearers part of a mass generation of protest. Such badges were the direct descendants of the stamped tin and copper alloy badges made in the 19th and 20th centuries as electioneering tools, to communicate political ideas, or as signs for the members and supporters of trade unionism and women's suffrage who had made deft use of brooches and badges in the purple, white and green of the movement to create a communal identity. Some early 20th-century suffrage campaigners wore a toffee-hammer-shaped brooch to commemorate the 1912 window-smashing campaign, while those who were jailed for their involvement in the cause were presented with the 'Holloway badge' in the form of a prison portcullis.

Badges could be made locally by anyone with basic equipment, such as the popular Badge-A-Minit, responding rapidly to social movements and needs, and giving a graphic identity to protest movements, followers of music bands and those who espoused counter-cultural views. A colourful collection of lapel badges (**133**) reveals a range of designs and subjects to be pinned to T-shirts and jeans jackets worn by young people in the 1970s.

CHAPTER EIGHT
'The shock of beauty'
1990–The Present

Jewellers at the end of the 20th century have used the pictorial surface offered by brooches to comment on social attitudes and politics, and to make personal statements. Recycled materials and found objects work alongside traditional materials interpreted in innovative ways to make jewels offering a statement on our world and our place in it.

Jan Yager's 'American Sidewalk' brooch resulted from examining the sidewalks around her Philadelphia studio, collecting the tough, adaptable plants that survive in the cracks of city buildings as well as the crack cocaine vials, bullet casings, cigarette butts and broken bottles testifying to the darker side of urban life. Her art reflects its time and place, with jewels that serve as reminders of the issues facing contemporary society (**135**).

Jonathan Boyd's brooch, titled 'All my own words and thoughts', is also inspired by the clutter of the city around him (**136**). He incorporates text, often in the form of metal typeset, to create jewels that examine how language and the city overlap. Here, the letters use the form of trademarks and fonts seen in the urban environment.

In the 1980s, Peter Chang began working with discarded plastics to make bold jewels in bright colours (**137**). Despite the low value of the material, his work was refined and immaculately finished, reflecting his training as a sculptor and printmaker. Turning away from precious metals, he used broken and disposable materials to create objects with their own value, explaining that, as well as enjoying the colours and tactile properties of acrylics, he liked 'the idea of working with a throwaway material which gives the freedom and luxury to make mistakes'.[1] Helen Britton's jewels often incorporate pieces reclaimed from old costume jewellery, her ethos fostered by childhood holidays in rural Australia and the 'make do and mend' ethic of her family.[2] Her vivid green flower brooch is made with green glass elements set in clear resin (**138**).

In Laurent Rivaud's brooch, gilded bullet cartridges set with glass stars hang underneath the embroidered letters 'FIRE' (**139**). Rivaud worked for the fashion designer Vivienne Westwood and shares some of her punk aesthetic. He made this jewel while running a masterclass at the Royal College of Arts in 2001, using low-cost materials to make a bold, provocative brooch.

The late 20th century saw many achievements in the struggle for sexual equality and a greater acceptance of differing sexual orientations, but was also scarred by the devastating impact of the AIDS epidemic. Keith Lewis's 'Peeling Off the Bitter Rind' brooch is a response to AIDS (**140**). It shows a gilded torso, the surface pitted like a citrus fruit, which has been peeled open to reveal metal innards. Lewis's work often refers to the male homosexual experience very directly, complicating the issue of the intended wearer of the brooch. Just as earlier political brooches affirmed allegiances, so contemporary brooches often require a willingness to make a public statement.

'Tom's Bar 2014' is a cheap plastic and metal badge which reproduces a stamp – an even more ephemeral object (**141**). The Finnish stamp is illustrated with a homoerotic design by the artist 'Tom of Finland' (Touko Laaksonen).

135 Oxidized silver, by Jan Yager. USA, 1999.
M.28-2001

136 Silver, by Jonathan Matthew Boyd. Scotland, 2015.
M.3-2016. Given by Jacqueline and Jonathan Gestetner

137 Acrylic and steel, by Peter Chang. Scotland, 2004.
M.25-2014. The Louise Klapisch Collection, given by Suzanne Selvi

138 Silver, resin, paint and glass, by Helen Britton. Germany, 2004.
M.23-2014. The Louise Klapisch Collection, given by Suzanne Selvi

139 Gilded metal, textile and glass, by Laurent Rivaud. London, 2001.
M.61-2007. Royal College of Art Visiting Artists Collection

140 Gilded silver, copper and steel brooch, by Keith Lewis. USA, 1993.
M.2-2014. Given in Honor of the Artist by the Porter Price Collection

After coming under fire from conservative Russian politicians opposed to LGBT rights, Finland's national TV station mailed letters with these stamps to Russia, in an act of protest and provocation. The badge therefore supports both gay rights and the desire to stress Finland's political and cultural independence from Russia, its former ruler.

Israeli jeweller Esther Knobel uses figures cut from old Chinese tea tins found in a Jerusalem antiques shop to make a seemingly playful reference to immigration, one of the century's great social preoccupations. She attempts to present a positive view: here, a rabbit wearing a flowered dress appears to be setting sail on an enamelled brooch (**142**). In a poem accompanying her 'Immigrants' brooches, Knobel describes them as a 'great commotion that can't be heard, but can be seen all too well', a throng on 'sail-shaped brooches with wheels, a Chinese circus, foreign workers, rabbits, rulers, families, children, cliques, individuals, and they're all wanderers'.[3]

Ramon Puig Cuyas also refers to travel in his 'Journal of Navigation', a brooch incorporating small metal elements reminiscent of archaeological remnants or flotsam and jetsam (**143**), while Peter Hoogeboom references the long history of Dutch colonial involvement in Asia in 'Street Vendor 4', a brooch of raffia and ceramic beads shaped like the lidded pots used by Asian street vendors (**144**).

Just as the badge could be used to express anti-establishment views or symbolize a protest movement, so wearing a brooch or flag pin could be used to cleave to more mainstream political views. In the 1970s, US President Richard Nixon and his supporters wore Stars and Stripes lapel pins to rebuke anti-Vietnam war protestors. In 2008, presidential candidate Barack Obama's questioning of 'people wearing a lapel pin but not acting very patriotic' was used to impugn his patriotism.[4] In China, loyalty to Chairman Mao was encouraged in the 1970s through wearing lapel pins with his image. They were created in enormous numbers in a variety

142 Tin, nickel silver and elastic, by Esther Knobel. Israel, 1987–90.
M.60-2014. The Louise Klapisch Collection, given by Suzanne Selvi

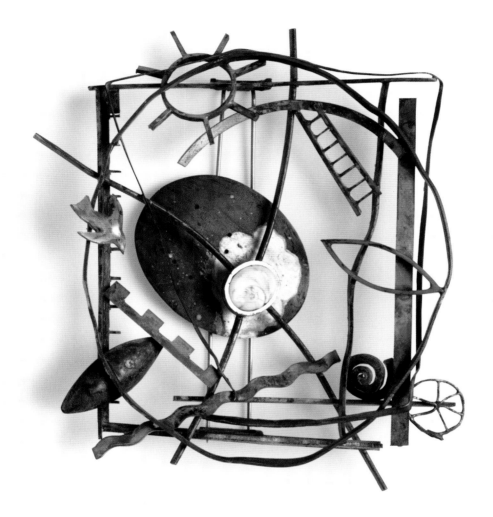

143 Oxidized silver, enamel and shell, by Ramon Puig Cuyas. Spain, 1995.
M.59:1-2014. The Louise Klapisch Collection, given by Suzanne Selvi

144 Ceramics, bamboo, silver and textile, by Peter Hoogeboom. Netherlands, 2009.
M.33-2014. The Louise Klapisch Collection, given by Suzanne Selvi

145 Group of Mao badges. China, 1960s.
FE 135-143-1988

of designs (**145**), to such a degree that excessive production diverted vital resources and used up the country's stock of aluminium.[5] Contemporary North Koreans are still required to wear a pin with the image of their president.

Madeleine Albright, the first female US Secretary of State, is famed for using brooches to convey subtle or sometimes very blunt messages (**146**). When called 'an unparalleled serpent' by the Iraqi president Saddam Hussein, she made a point of wearing an antique snake brooch to their next meeting. Butterfly and balloon brooches were chosen in moments of optimism; wasps, crabs and turtles when matters were moving less smoothly.

Contemporary jewellers have also explored a variety of materials and methods. Harold O'Connor's brooch in cow bone (**147**) harks back to the ancient tradition of using jewellery as an amulet to avert evil and protect the wearer. Set with gold and pierced with a metal

wire, it references the sacred medicine bundle carried by a Native American healer.

Platinum, with its strength and resistance to tarnish, has been highly valued since the 19th century and, as one of the most expensive metals, was principally used in fine settings for gemstones. The company Ayrton Metals encouraged its wider use by jewellers with a series of competitions running from 1979 to 1994. Karla Moon won first prize with a swooping brooch made using a newly developed metal-pressing technique (**148**).

The first gold brooch made by Jacqueline Ryan after graduating from art college shows her desire to make jewels that are 'the essence of nature captured and translated into a finished, wearable piece of jewellery' (**149**).[6] Each petal is individually forged, pierced and soldered. Giovanni Corvaja's hexagonal brooch, meanwhile, has a fairy-like delicacy (**150**). The geometric gold structure of the brooch is filled

146 Madeleine Albright wearing an American eagle pin at the Democratic National Convention, Wells Fargo Center, Philadelphia, Pennsylvania, USA, 2016.
Photo: Paul Morigi/WireImage via Getty Images

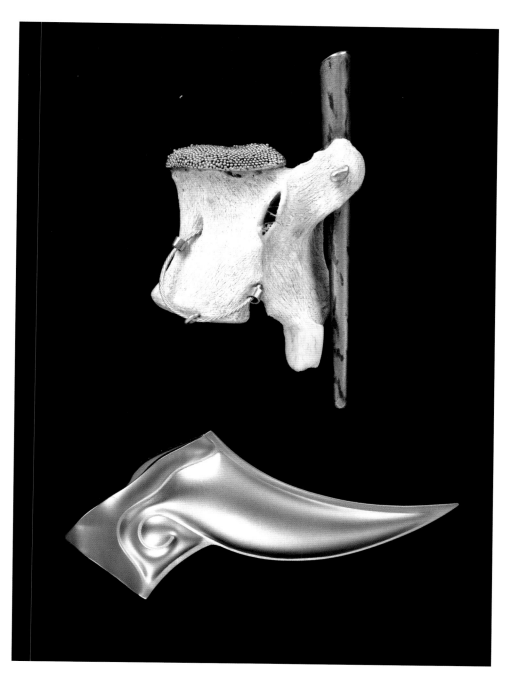

147 Cow bone, gold and silver, by Harold O'Connor. USA, 1996.
M.30-2006. Given by Martha Connell
148 Platinum, by Karla Moon. London, 1987.
M.19-1995

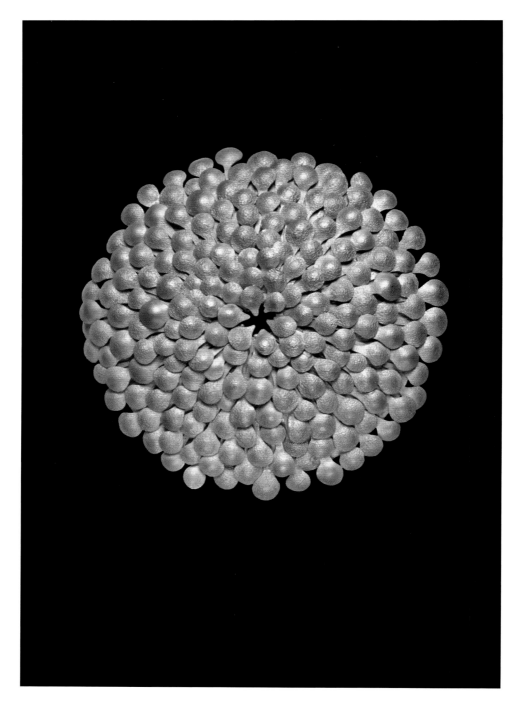

149 Gold, by Jacqueline Ryan. Italy, 1994.
M.44-2014. The Louise Klapisch Collection, given by Suzanne Selvi

150 Gold and platinum, by Giovanni Corvaja. Italy, 2000.
M.5-2004

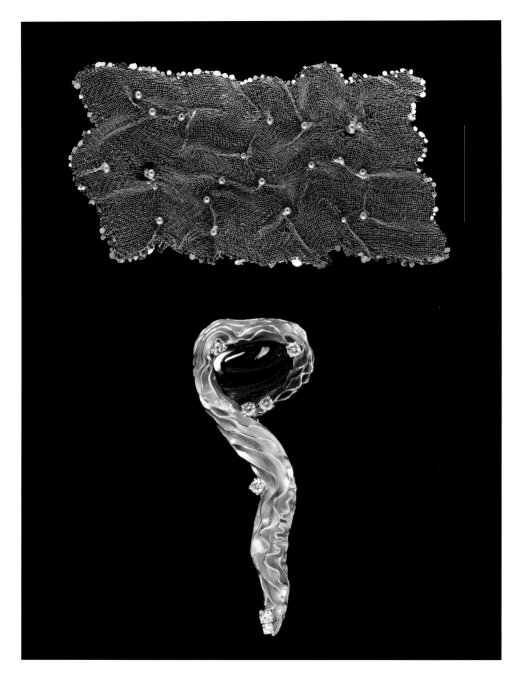

151 Platinum gauze and gold, by Jacqueline Mina. London, 1996.
M.19-2013. Given by Katherine Purcell through the Art Fund

152 Gold, amethyst and diamonds, by Mario Saba. London, c.1994.
M.32-1999. Given by Katrine Saba

with fine platinum filaments decorated with granules of gold. Corvaja studied in Padua, the centre of Italian goldsmithing, mastering traditional techniques as well as inventing his own tools and methods, which have included drawing wire to a fineness of less than 10 microns. In a 2016 interview, he described his desire to make jewellery that attracted attention through the 'shock of beauty' rather than by making a provocative statement.[7]

Jacqueline Mina also used platinum and granules of gold to make a brooch with a decidedly textile effect (**151**). When she applied to the Royal College of Art in the 1960s, the silversmithing course did not accept women, so she decided to study jewellery. Most of her work is in gold but in the 1990s Ayrton Metals invited her to explore platinum. They supplied her with platinum gauze made for the chemical industries, which she experimented with to create an irregular appearance. Small, soldered gold

granules both define the design and strengthen the structure.

Mario Saba's gold and carved amethyst brooch uses the technical skills he developed while apprenticed to Bulgari, the Italian jewellery house (**152**). In 1980, Saba set up his own premises on London's Sloane Street. He wanted 'a craftsman's shop, with a workshop downstairs where I was manufacturing. It was probably one of the first craftsman's shops in London, where people could come along and I could set their loose stones and produce jewellery especially for my clients.'[8] The organic, flowing goldwork is created by casting from a model made with hot wax extruded through a tube to create swirling ribbons, a process Saba developed in the 1990s.

David Watkins was, for almost twenty years, a professor at the Royal College of Art. He began his career in the 1960s as a sculptor, jazz pianist

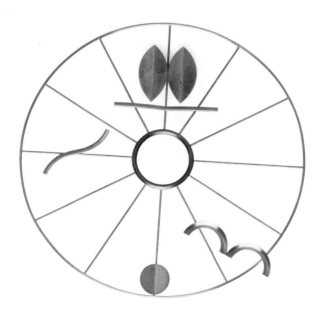

153 Yellow and white gold, by David Watkins. London, 1998.
M.12-2010. Supported by the Friends of the V&A

154 Oxidized silver and coral, by Dorothy Hogg. Scotland, 2008.
M.32-2014. The Louise Klapisch Collection, given by Suzanne Selvi

155 Acrylic and oxidized silver, by Barbara Paganin. Italy, 2011.
M.226:1-2011. Given by the Friends of the V&A

156 Silver, gold and enamel, by Ike Jünger. Germany, 2010.
M.22-2010

157 Silver, by Julie Blyfield. Australia, 2007.
M.21-2014. The Louise Klapisch Collection, given by Suzanne Selvi

and special-effects model maker, notably making model spaceships for Stanley Kubrick's 1968 film *2001: A Space Odyssey*. He has explored a wide range of media, from paper to gold, and industrial materials such as acrylic, steel, aluminium and titanium. An early exponent of computer-aided design, he created work in the 1990s – including the 'Wheel Pin' series – that is characterized by a return to gold and experiments with 3D computer modelling (**153**).

Dorothy Hogg's jewels are often based on hollow forms, giving each piece an essential lightness. Her jewellery is inspired both by the way in which a piece interacts with the body

and by the body itself. The brooch shown here (**154**) is part of the 'Artery' series, a group of jewels in which silver, oxidized to a grey colour, contrasts with blood-red felt or coral.

Barbara Paganin used dental acrylic to cast directly from a head of Romanesco broccoli to create a large brooch whose irregular silver base follows the contour of the cast. The naturalism of the fractal patterns found on the surface of the broccoli is offset by the orange colour of the acrylic, contrasting realism with artifice (**155**). Ike Jünger's sensitive use of enamel on curls of silver sheet creates a brooch that imitates tree bark with an almost photorealistic degree of detail (**156**). Julie Blyfield's

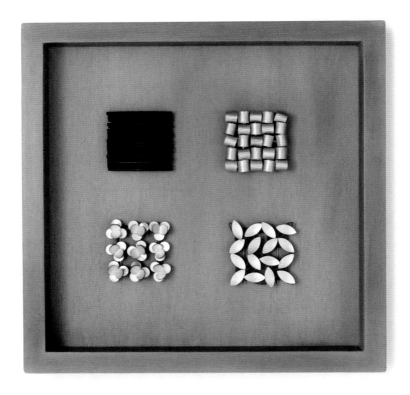

158 Gold, silver, oxidized silver, mother-of-pearl and stainless steel, by Anna Gordon. Scotland, 2017.
M.36 to 39-2017

'Paperseed' brooch is inspired by the flora of her native Australia, with the intention not 'to replicate plant forms in a botanically correct fashion, but ... to capture the essence of the things I discover' (**157**).⁹ Anna Gordon's set of brooches, 'The Four gentlemen of China', demonstrates both her love of nature and her interest in formal and repeating patterns (**158**). The 'Four gentlemen' in traditional Asian art refer to the orchid, bamboo, chrysanthemum and plum blossom, where each plant represents a season.

Jack Cunningham uses the language of readymades and collage, which was pioneered in the early 20th century by Picasso, Braque and Duchamp, to make a colourful, playful brooch (**159**). It is based on the riddling Scottish rhyme traditionally associated with the coat of arms of his home town, Glasgow:

Here's the bird that never flew,
Here's the tree that never grew,
Here's the bell that never rang,
Here's the fish that never swam.

Meanwhile, Bettina Speckner's brooch (**160**) is based on sections of Baroque scrolls that have been joined together. The precise crafting of Speckner's brooch contrasts with the organic folds of Ruudt Peters's 'ANIMA – Emalia' (**161**), in which the shape is created by allowing swirls

159 White metal, cornelian, wood, paint and ready-mades, by Jack Cunningham. Scotland, 2005.
M.32-2017

160 Gold, by Bettina Speckner. London, 2001.
M.62-2007. Royal College of Art Visiting Artists Collection

161 Electroformed and gilded silver, by Ruudt Peters. Netherlands, 2009.
M.23-2010

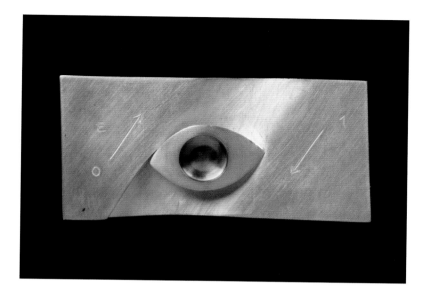

of molten wax to cool in moving water. Peters wanted to explore Carl Jung's theory of the 'anima', the idea that each person has both a female and a male side. Working with wax made 'a flowing line captured in solidified form'[10] – a kind of 'blind drawing' that allowed him to free his creativity and access his female subconscious.

Bruno Martinazzi's brooch, though minimalist in design, carries a philosophical and symbolic charge (**162**). He describes his jewellery as capturing gestures, signs and signals to make them immortal. The eye in the centre represents a window to the soul. It is flanked by arrows relating to the numbers 0 and 1 and the letter E, representing energy. It was inspired by learning about Professor Sydney Leach's research into

laser energy and the radiation emitted by stars. As Martinazzi explained: 'What fascinated me was the way energy went from zero level to level one. This leap was fantastic; zero is absolutely nothing, one, on the other hand is everything, the beginning of everything.'[11]

The advantages of a conversation-provoking brooch or pin are many. Contemporary designers are exploring their possibilities, whether as a silk flower on a man's jacket, conceived as an 'icebreaker' accessory worn by a 'gentleman, who immediately appears more creative and stylish without being "de trop"',[12] or an oversized Burberry lapel pin (see **134**), worn first in an advertising campaign but perhaps ready to find its place in the mainstream fashion of the near future.

162 Gold, by Bruno Martinazzi. London, 1992.
M.33-2007. Royal College of Art Visiting Artists Collection

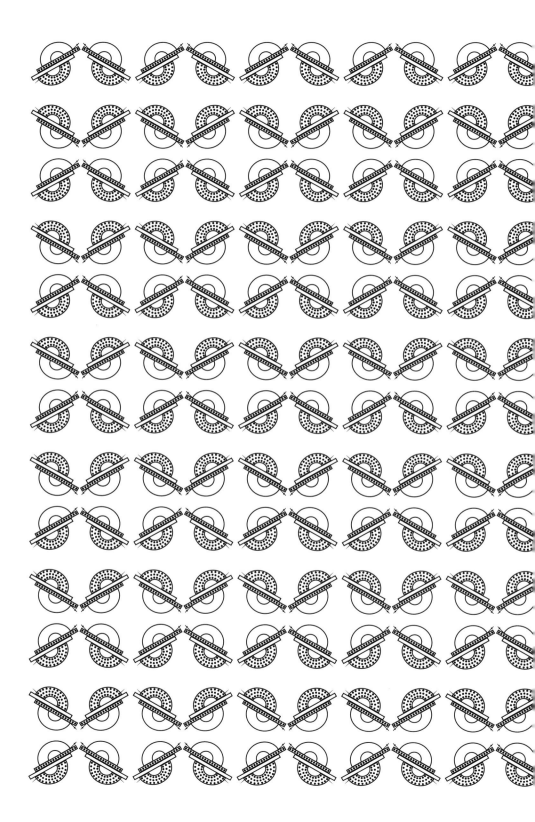

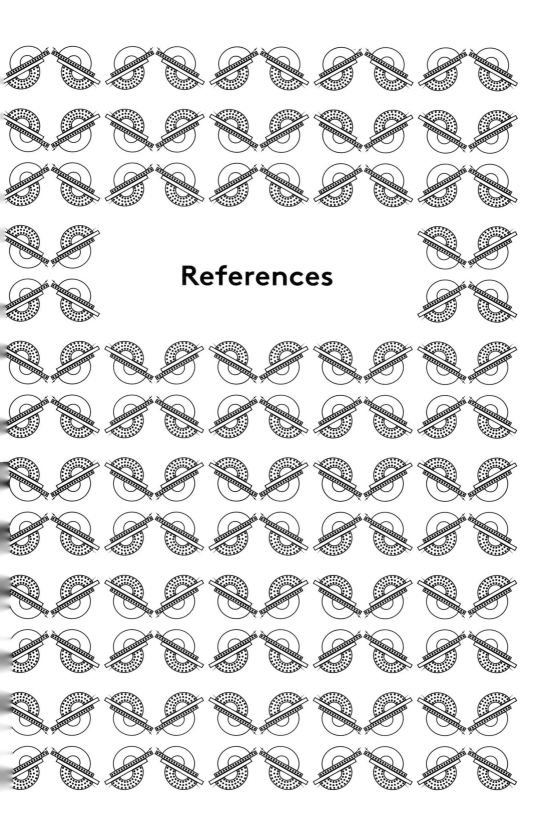

References

Glossary

Baguette cut a step-cut gemstone in a long rectangular shape

Brilliant cut a round diamond cut with 58 facets, 33 on the crown (or upper) section of the stone and 25 on the pavilion (or lower) section. In general use by the 19th century, a brilliant cut is characterized by its superior brilliancy.

Cabochon a stone that has been polished smooth rather than cut into facets

Clip brooch a brooch that is fastened by pinching a layer of fabric between the clip and the body of the brooch

Collet a metal band or setting to hold a stone in place

Enamel a substance formed from coloured glass powder fused onto a metallic surface

Engraving cutting patterns or lettering into metal with sharp tools

Granulation decorative technique consisting of fixing minute balls of gold to a metal surface

Latten an alloy of copper and zinc, resembling brass

Lost-wax casting a method of creating a mould by setting a wax model in a material such as clay or plaster and then melting the wax to create a void into which metal can be poured. When the metal hardens, the mould is broken to release the object.

Micromosaic a design made of very small hardstone, enamel or glass pieces in a metal frame

Niello a black mixture of copper, silver and lead sulphides inlaid into engraved metal

Oxidized silver silver with a surface intentionally blackened with a sulphide compound

Paste substitute for gemstones, made from a glass compound

Pavé set small gemstones very closely set with tiny metal prongs

Ring brooch brooch fastened by passing a central pin through a loosely woven fabric and using the weight of the fabric to hold it in place

Rose cut a pointed diamond cut with a flat base, often made up of 24 triangular facets. Developed before the brilliant cut, the rose cut involves less wastage of stone, but achieves less sparkle.

Silver-gilt silver coated with a fine layer of gold

Table cut one of the earliest styles of gem cutting, in which the upper part of the stone is removed to leave a large rectangular facet surrounded by a bevelled edge or smaller facets

Further Reading

Albright, Madeleine and Elaine Shocas, *Read My Pins: Stories from a Diplomat's Jewel Box* (New York, 2009)

Angulo, Lorena, *Behind the Brooch: A Closer Look at Backs, Catches, and Pin Stems* (Atglen, PA, 2014)

Attwood, Philip, *Badges* (London, 2004)

Campbell, Marian, *Medieval Jewellery in Europe 1100–1500* (London, 2009)

Deevy, Mary B., *Medieval Ring Brooches in Ireland* (Dublin, 1998)

Drutt, Helen W., *Brooching it Diplomatically: A Tribute to Madeleine K. Albright* (Stuttgart, 2001)

Estrada, Nicolas, *New Brooches: 400+ Contemporary Jewellery Designs* (Barcelona, 2018)

Ettlinger Gross, Lori, *Brooches: Timeless Adornment* (New York, 2008)

Hattatt, Richard, *A Visual Catalogue of Richard Hattatt's Ancient Brooches* (Oxford, 2000)

Le Van, Marthe, *500 Brooches: Inspiring Adornments for the Body* (Asheville, NC, 2005)

Lightbown, Ronald W., *Mediaeval European Jewellery: With a Catalogue of the Collection in the Victoria & Albert Museum* (London, 1992)

Martin, Paul, *The Trade Union Badge: Material Culture in Action* (Aldershot, 2002)

Martin, Toby F., *The Cruciform Brooch and Anglo-Saxon England* (Woodbridge, 2015)

Mitchiner, Michael, *Medieval Pilgrim and Secular Badges* (London, 1986)

Phillips, Clare, *Jewels and Jewellery* (London, 2019)

Sequin, Ken, *The Graphic Art of the Enamel Badge* (London, 1999)

Spencer, Brian, *Pilgrim Souvenirs and Secular Badges: Medieval Finds from Excavations in London* (London, 1998)

Turrell, Elizabeth, *The Enamel Experience: International Badge Exhibition* (Bristol, 2007)

Wang, Helen, *Chairman Mao Badges: Symbols and Slogans of the Cultural Revolution* (London, 2008)

Notes

Introduction

1 'Advertising Jewellery', *Goldsmiths' Journal*, Nov. 1926, p. 240

Chapter One: 1100–1500

1 Mary Deevy, 'Ring brooches in Medieval Ireland', *Archaeology Ireland*, vol. 10, no. 2 (Summer 1996), pp. 8–10; Deevy, *Medieval Ring Brooches in Ireland*, 1998, pls. 32–4

2 'Le Dit du Mercier', quoted in Lightbown, *Mediaeval European Jewellery*, 1992, p. 53

3 William Langland, *The Vision and Creed of Piers Ploughman*, ed. B. Thomas Wright (London, 1856), p. 29, v. 907

4 John Heywood, *The Playe Called the Foure PP*, London, 1544

5 Geoffrey Chaucer, 'The Legend of Good Women' in *The Poetical Works of Geoffrey Chaucer*, ed. Robert Bell (London, 1856), p. 83

6 Laura F. Hodges, *Chaucer and Array: Patterns of Costume and Fabric Rhetoric in the Canterbury Tales, Troilus and Criseyde and Other Works* (Cambridge, 2014), pp. 75–9; Hodges, 'Sartorial Signs in "Troilus and Criseyde"', *The Chaucer Review*, vol. 35, no. 3, 2001, pp. 223–59

7 British Museum inventory number 1929,0411.1

8 Quoted in Lightbown, *Mediaeval European Jewellery*, 1992, p. 138

9 Quoted in Campbell, *Medieval Jewellery in Europe*, 2009, p. 96

10 Jean Renart, *The Romance of the Rose or Guillaume de Dole*, ed. N.V. Durling and P. Terry (Philadelphia, 1993), quoted in Deevy, *Medieval Ring Brooches in Ireland*, 1998, p. 63

11 Laura F. Hodges, *Chaucer and Clothing: Clerical and Academic Costume in the General Prologue to the Canterbury Tales* (Cambridge, 2005), p. 119

12 Caesarius of Heisterbach, quoted in Don C. Skemer, *Binding Words: Textual Amulets in the Middle Ages* (Pennsylvania, 2010), p. 92

13 Annemarieke Willemsen, '"Man is a sack of muck girded with silver": Metal Decoration on Late-medieval Leather Belts and Purses from the Netherlands', *Medieval Archaeology*, vol. 56, 2012, pp. 171–201

14 Lightbown, *Mediaeval European Jewellery*, 1992, pp. 152–3, fig. 87 and p. 183

15 Nigel Saul, 'The Commons and the Abolition of Badges', *Parliamentary History*, 9, pp. 302–15

Chapter Two: 1500–1800

1 From Nicholas Breton, *The Court and the Country* (London, 1618)

2 William Harrison, *The Description of England* (Ithaca, 1968), p. 231

3 Benvenuto Cellini, *La Vita* (1973 edition), book 1, p. xxxi, quoted in Natasha Awais-Dean, *Bejewelled: Men and Jewellery in Tudor and Jacobean England* (London, 2017), p. 46

4 Discussed in Awais-Dean, 2017, pp. 59–63

5 Rosalind K. Marshall and George R. Dalgleish (eds.), *The Art of Jewellery in Scotland* (Edinburgh, 1991), p. 13

6 Daniel Cramer, *Emblemata Sacra*, 1624, Decas V

7 Pierre Erondelle, *The French Garden: For English Ladyes and Gentlewomen to Walke In...* (1605), Dialogue 10

8 Quoted in Nichola Erin Harris, 'The Idea of Lapidary Medicine: Its Circulation and Practical Applications in Medieval and Early Modern England 1000–1750', Rutgers University PhD dissertation, 2009, p. 185

9 BL Sloane 2539 (British Library), quoted in Harris (2009), p. 156

10 Joanna Whalley, 'Smoke and Mirrors: The Enhancement and Simulation of Gemstones in Renaissance Europe' in *The Renaissance Workshop* (London, 2013), pp. 79–89

11 David Jeffries, *A Treatise on diamonds and pearls: in which their importance is considered: and plain rules are exhibited for ascertaining the value of both; and the true method of manufacturing diamonds* (London, 1751), p. 66

12 *The Spectator*, vol. 2, no. 270, Wednesday, January 7, 1712

13 Jeffries (cited note 11), p. 66

14 Hazel Forsyth, *The Cheapside Hoard: London's Lost Jewels* (London, 2014), pp. 134–6

15 Monique Rakhorst, 'Bow Jewels of the Golden Age: In Fashion in the Low Countries', *The Rijksmuseum Bulletin*, no. 1, 2018, pp. 4–23

16 Antoine Furetière, *Dictionnaire universel, contenant généralement tous les mots françois [sic] tant vieux que modernes, et les termes de toutes les sciences et des arts* (1690)

17 Olga W. Gorewa et al., *Joyaux du trésor de Russie* (Paris, 1990), p. 51

18 W.B. Gerard, *Laurence Sterne and the Visual Imagination* (Aldershot, 2006), p. 147

19 Marshall and Dalgleish (cited note 5), p. 41

Chapter Three: 1800–1900

1 Elizabeth Gaskell, *Cranford* (Leipzig, 1867), p. 139

2 'Violet Hamilton, or The Talented Family', *Tait's Edinburgh Magazine* (1840), vol. VII, p. 459

3 Catherine Taylor, 'Letters from Italy to a Younger Sister', *Tait's Edinburgh Magazine* (1840), vol. VII, p. 737

4 Ibid.

5 Joseph Severn's image of Ariel (1826), captioned 'On the Bat's Back I Do Fly', was used in Charles Knight (ed.), *The Pictorial Edition of the Works of Shakespeare, Comedies*, vol. II, (London, 1839–42), ill. 2, p. 389

6 Charlotte Gere and Judy Rudoe, *Jewellery in the Age of Queen Victoria: A Mirror to the World* (London, 2010), p. 467

7 *Princely Magnificence: Court Jewels of the Renaissance, 1500–1630*, Jill Hollis (ed.), exhibition catalogue, Victoria and Albert Museum, 15 Oct. 1980–1 Feb. 1981 (London, 1980), p. 133, cat. H2

8 'On the Present State of the Arts in Italy', *The Saturday Magazine* (9 December 1843), vols. 22–3, no. 734, p. 227

9 Ibid.

10 Susan Weber Soros and Stefanie Walker, *Castellani and Italian Archaeological Jewellery* (New York, 2004), p. 231

11 Print by Lodovico Pogliaghi, quoted in Lucia Pirzio-Biroli Stefanelli, 'Dogali, January 1887: an engraved sapphire by Giorgio Antonio Girardet for a Castellani brooch', *Burlington Magazine* (June 2002), pp. 354–6

12 *The Jeweller and Fancy Trades Advertiser* (April 1868), p. 119

13 Old Bailey Proceedings Online (accessed 19 June 2018): October 1815, trial of Margaret Power (t18151025-119)

14 Gaskell (cited note 1), p. 254

15 Quoted in Mary Peter, *Collecting Victorian Jewellery* (London, 1970), p. 88

16 Kevin Desmond, *Gustave Trouvé: French Electrical Genius (1839–1902)* (Jefferson, NC, 2015), p. 44

17 *Vogue* (5 August 1893), vol. 2, iss. 6, S.4

18 *Public Opinion* (1904), p. 752

19 *Vogue* (8 August 1895), vol. 6, iss. 6, p. iii

20 *Vogue* (10 December 1896), vol. 8, iss. 23, p. xxiv

21 *Vogue* (15 April 1897), vol. 9, iss. 15, p. 234

22 'On Female Hair', *Ladies Cabinet of Fashion, Music and Romance* (1847), p. 309

23 *Ladies Home Journal* (December 1892), 10, no. 1, p. 8

24 *The Jewellers, Goldsmiths and Watchmakers' Monthly Magazine* (1862), pp. 116–18

25 *Vogue* (1 August 1895), vol. 6, iss. 5, p. 75

26 Henri Vever, *French Jewelry of the Nineteenth Century* (London, 2001), p. 1009

Chapter Four: 1900–1920

1 Henri Vever, 'Boucles de ceinture', *Art et Décoration* (January 1898), p. 157

2 Henri Vever, *French Jewelry of the Nineteenth Century* (London, 2001), p. 1247

3 Yvonne Brunhammer (ed.), *The Jewels of Lalique* (Paris, 1998), p. 10

4 Ibid., p. 130

5 Alphonse Fouquet, quoted in Marie-Nöel De Gary, *Les Fouquet: Bijoutiers et Joailliers à Paris 1860–1960* (Paris, 1983), p. 9

6 Henri Vever, 'Les bijoux aux Salons de 1898', *Art et Décoration* (January 1898), p. 169

7 'L'exposition des artistes décorateurs au Pavillon de Marsan', *Art et Décoration* (July 1906), pp. 199–200

8 Ibid.

9 Alphonse Mucha, *Documents Décoratifs* (Paris, 1902–3), p. 5

10 *Vogue* (8 February 1900), vol. 15, iss. 6, p. 93

11 M.P. Verneuil, 'L'exposition des arts et métiers de la Grande Bretagne au Pavillon de Marsan', *Art et Décoration* (January 1914), p. 158

12 Interview by Harriet Monroe, 'An Experiment in Jewelry', *House Beautiful* (July 1900), quoted by Laura Mathews in 'Sapphires and Suffragettes: The Unsinkable Mrs. William H. Klapp' (online; accessed 14 March 2018)

13 Quoted in Cassidy Zachary, 'Revisiting the Art of the Peacock: A Golden Age, Fashion & Fantasy, 1894–1920, Part One' (27 February 2015) (online, accessed 13 March 2018)

14 Ann Dumas, 'Victorian Modern: The Metalwork Designs of Christopher Dresser, C.R. Ashbee and Archibald Knox 1889–1910', *The Magazine Antiques* (June 1985), vol. 127, p. 1347

15 Felicity Ashbee, *Janet Ashbee: Love, Marriage and the Arts and Crafts Movement* (Syracuse, NY, 2002), p. 58

16 'In memoriam: Reginald Oswald Pearson', *The Apple (of Beauty and of Discord)*, 1920, p. 174

17 Delia Austrian, 'Sisters of the Arts and Crafts', *Technical World Magazine* (October 1906), vol. 6, no. 2, p. 172

18 Gustave Geffroy, 'Des bijoux. A propos de M. René Lalique', *Art et Décoration* (July 1905), p. 179

19 *Vogue* (22 February 1900), vol. 15, iss. 8, p. 126

20 'Famous Swordsman', *Evening Post* (New Zealand, 18 February 1911), vol. LXXXI, iss. 41, p. 4

21 *Vogue* (15 April 1911), vol. 37, iss. 8, p. 53

22 Robert Carsix, 'Bijoux dessinés par Iribe', *Art et Décoration* (January 1911), pp. 31–2

23 'The War Exerts its Influence on Jewellery', *Vogue* (1 February 1918), vol. 51, iss. 3, p. 64

Chapter Five: 1920–1940

1 *Goldsmiths' Journal* (November 1926), vol. XV, p. 222

2 *The New Yorker* (25 November 1939), p. 70

3 *The New Yorker* (2 December 1933), p. 76

4 *The New Yorker* (30 December 1932), p. 64

5 'The Modern Craving for Colour', *Goldsmiths' Journal* (April 1927), vol. XIV, iss. 98, p. 93

6 'The Jewels of the Moderns', *Vogue* (1 August 1924), vol. 64, iss. 3, p. 42

7 'The Modern Craving for Colour' (cited note 5), p. 94

8 *The New Yorker* (28 December 1929), p. 53

9 Advertisement for Tecla jewels, *The New Yorker* (14 December 1929), p. 4

10 *The New Yorker* (3 December 1927), p. 89

11 *The New Yorker* (8 December 1934), p. 127

12 *The New Yorker* (2 December 1933), p. 76

13 *The New Yorker* (8 December 1934), p. 129

14 'The Modern Craving for Colour' (cited note 5), p. 94

15 *Studio* magazine, 1929, quoted in Clare Phillips, 'Art Deco Jewellery', in *Art Deco: 1910–1939*, ed. Charlotte Benton et al. (London, 2003), p. 276

16 'The Paris Mode at the Races', *Vogue* (15 December 1923), vol. 62, iss. 12, p. 98

17 *The New Yorker* (29 November 1930), p. 63

18 *Goldsmiths' Journal* (November 1930), p. 250

19 Quoted in Sylvie Raulet, *Bijoux Art Deco* (Paris, 1984), p. 173

20 Gaston Varenne, 'Raymond Templier et le bijou moderne', *Art et Décoration* (February 1930), p. 57

21 Quoted in Raulet (cited note 19), p. 76

22 *Goldsmiths' Journal* (March 1930), p. 765

23 *The New Yorker* (7 December 1935), p. 84

24 *Sheffield Daily Independent*, quoted in the *Goldsmiths' Journal* (May 1938), no. 231, p. 144

25 *The Gemmologist* (March 1938), p. 651

Chapter Six: 1940–1960

1 'Fashion: Scotch that Rumour – Here's the Truth: Gloves Are Going…Going/Jewellery will be Frozen…', *Vogue* (New York, 1 February 1943), vol. 101, iss. 3, p. 115

2 From 1 January 1939 all gold was under the control of the Überwachungsstelle für Edelmetalle (Monitoring Centre for Precious Metals), to whom jewellers had to apply for a quota of gold.

3 *The New Yorker* (20 November 1943), p. 70

4 *Goldsmiths' Journal* (February 1939), p. 529

5 *The New Yorker* (23 November 1940), p. 75

6 *Vogue* (1 September 1940), vol. 96, iss. 5, p. 105

7 *The New Yorker* (10 December 1949), pp. 79–82

8 *The New Yorker* (17 November 1951), p. 151

9 *Femina* (May 1945), p. 49

10 *The New Yorker* (15 November 1952), p. 142

11 *The New Yorker* (10 November 1956), p. 181

12 *The New Yorker* (6 December 1941), p. 110

13 Sally Everitt and David Lancaster, *Christie's Twentieth Century Jewellery* (London, 2002), p. 90

14 *Vogue* (15 October 1959), vol. 134, iss. 7, p. 85

15 *The New Yorker* (10 November 1956), p. 173

16 *The New Yorker* (17 November 1951), p. 150

17 *The New Yorker* (7 October 1961), p. 95

18 Quoted in Christianne Weber and Renate Möller, *Mode und Modeschmuck / Fashion and Jewelry 1920–1970* (Stuttgart, 1999), p. 137

19 *Design Quarterly*, No. 45/46, American Jewelry (1959), p. 56

20 *The New Yorker* (21 December 1940), p. 6

21 *Media Arts Magazine*, quoted in Barbara Cartlidge, *Twentieth-Century Jewelry* (New York, 1985), p. 75

22 Advertisement for De Beers diamonds in *The New Yorker* (10 February 1962), p. 5

Chapter Seven: 1960–1990

1 *The New Yorker* (16 November 1957), p. 183

2 John Donald and Russell Cassleton Elliott, *Precious Statements* (Carmarthen, 2015), p. 141

3 Jacob E. Nyenhuis, *Myth and the Creative Process: Michael Ayrton and the Myth of Daedalus the Maze Maker* (Detroit, 2003), p. 139

4 Michael Ayrton, *The Maze Maker* (Chicago, 1967), p. 181

5 Craft Lives interview, 2006, British Library sound archive (C960/73) (accessed 25 May 2018)

6 Ralph Turner, *Jewelry in Europe and America: New Times, New Thinking* (London, 1996), p. 22

7 Foreword, 'International Exhibition of Modern Jewellery 1890–1961' catalogue (Kent, 1961), n.p.

8 Cathleen McCarthy, interview with Helen Drutt, 5 February 2013 (online, accessed 10 April 2018)

9 'Susanna Heron Jewellery, The First Decade 1971–1982' (online, accessed 11 April 2018)

10 Robert Ebendorf, 'Elsa Freund on Elsaramic Jewelry' (online, accessed 25 May 2018)

11 Artist note, Smithsonian American Art Museum (online, accessed 25 May 2018)

12 Lindsay Pollock, exhibition review, 'Thomas Gentille: Twenty-First Century', Art Jewelry Forum, 19 November 2010 (online, accessed 25 May 2018)

13 Arline Fisch interview for the Archives of American Art, the Smithsonian Institution (online, accessed 30 May 2018)

14 Press release for exhibition 'Artists in Treasured Jewelry', Orlando Museum of Art, Florida, 2008

15 Quoted in Jeannine Falino, 'Diamonds Were the Badge of the Philistines, Art Jewelry at Midcentury', *Metalsmith* (2011), vol. 30, no. 5, p. 50

16 'Andrew Logan's Alternative Miss World', *Accent* (13 March 2017), iss. 2

Chapter Eight: 1990–The Present

1 'A Sense of Jewellery: Rediscovering British Jewellery Design' catalogue, 15 September–19 November 2015, The Goldsmiths' Centre, London

2 Damian Skinner and Kevin Murray, *Place and Adornment: A History of Contemporary Jewellery in Australia and New Zealand* (Auckland, 2014), pp. 176–7

3 Esther Knobel, 'The Mind in the Hand' (Tel Aviv, 2008), n.p.

4 Gilbert Cruz, 'A brief history of the flag pin', *Time* magazine, 3 July 2008

5 Attwood, *Badges*, 2004, p. 38

6 'From Black to Gold' catalogue, The Scottish Gallery (online, accessed 26 July 2018)

7 'Interview with Italian Goldsmith Giovanni Corvaja' by Barb Bauer, Spring 2016 (online, accessed 4 June 2018)

8 'A Twist of Fate', *Jewellery International*, Oct./Nov. 1994, pp. 67–8

9 Susan Cummins, 'Julie Blyfield: Second Nature, Gallery Funaki, Melbourne, AU', Art Jewelry Forum, 15 March 2013 (online, accessed 8 June 2018)

10 Artist statement for Ornamentum Gallery, March 2010

11 Carla Gallo Barbisio, 'Bruno Martinazzi, Schmuck – Gioelli – Jewellery' (Stuttgart, 1997), p. 109

12 Christian Barker, 'Cinabre Paris' Sartorial Icebreakers', *The Rake*, April 2018 (online, accessed 14 June 2018)

Major Collections Featuring Brooches and Badges

Boston Museum of Fine Arts, Boston, Massachusetts, USA

British Museum, London, UK

The Metropolitan Museum of Art and The Met Cloisters, New York, USA

Musée de Cluny – Musée national du Moyen Âge, Paris, France

Musée des Arts Décoratifs, Paris, France

Musée du Louvre, Paris, France

Museo Nazionale del Bargello, Florence, Italy

Museum of London, London, UK

National Museum of Ireland, Dublin, Ireland

National Museum of Scotland, Edinburgh, UK

National Museum of Wales, Cardiff, UK

Nordiska Museet, Stockholm, Sweden

Schmuckmuseum, Pforzheim, Germany

State Diamond Fund, Kremlin, Moscow, Russia

Victoria and Albert Museum, London, UK

Acknowledgments

I owe thanks to many people, not least to Richard Edgcumbe and Clare Phillips for their generosity and wisdom, to Joanna Whalley for gemmological and jewellery advice, to the V&A Photographic Studio, and in particular Richard Davis and Christine Smith. Marian Campbell's advice on medieval brooches was invaluable, as was Susan North's help with men's shirts and brooches. I am grateful to Ava McKenzie Welch for checking captions and images. Many thanks to Hannah Newell for being an understanding and forbearing editor, and to the Thames & Hudson publication team. Thank you to Paul, Oscar and Miranda for living through the pains and pleasures of brooches and badges with me. Above all, I would like to thank William and Judith Bollinger for their unwavering support for the Victoria and Albert Museum's Jewellery Gallery and collection.

Author's Biography

Rachel Church is a Curator in the Sculpture, Metalwork, Ceramics and Glass Department at the Victoria and Albert Museum. She has lectured and published on rings and general jewellery, and was part of the team that redisplayed the William and Judith Bollinger Jewellery Gallery at the Museum. Her publications include *Rings* (2011, republished 2017).

Index

Page numbers in *italics* refer to illustrations

Frontispiece: Gold, brilliant-cut diamond and miniature painting; jewellery by Frédéric Boucheron, painting by Fernand Paillet. Paris, c.1890.
M.171-1976. Bequeathed by Miss Julie Gollan through the Art Fund

pp. 6–7: Figures wearing brooches to pin clothing at the neck, breast and hip. Triptych in enamel and copper, by the Master of the Louis XII Triptych. Limoges, France, c.1498–1514.
552-1877

First published in the United Kingdom in 2019 by Thames & Hudson Ltd, London, in association with the Victoria and Albert Museum, London

Brooches and Badges © 2019 Victoria and Albert Museum, London/Thames & Hudson Ltd, London

Text and V&A photographs © 2019 Victoria and Albert Museum, London

Design and layout © 2019 Thames & Hudson Ltd, London

Designed by Angela Won-Yin Mak

British Library Cataloguing-in-Publication Data

A catalogue record for this book is available from the British Library

ISBN 978-0-500-48035-9

Printed and bound in China by 1010 Printing International Ltd

To find out about all our publications, please visit **www.thamesandhudson.com**. There you can subscribe to our e-newsletter, browse or download our current catalogue, and buy any titles that are in print.

MIX
Paper from responsible sources
FSC™ C016973
www.fsc.org

V&A Publishing

Supporting the world's leading museum of art and design, the Victoria and Albert Museum, London